THE SOUTHERN
COOKIE
BOOK

Published by Oxmoor House, an imprint of Time Inc. Books
225 Liberty Street, New York, NY 10281

Senior Editor: Katherine Cobbs
Editorial Assistants: Nicole Fisher, April Smitherman
Assistant Managing Editor: Jeanne de Lathouder
Assistant Project Editor: Lauren Moriarty
Senior Designer: Maribeth Jones
Junior Designer: AnnaMaria Jacob
Photographers: Iain Bagwell, Victor Protasio
Prop Stylists: Kay E. Clarke, Mindi Shapiro Levine, Lydia DeGaris Pursell
Hand Model: Kylie Dazzo
Food Stylists: Victoria E. Cox, Margaret Monroe Dickey, Rishon Hanners, Catherine Crowell Steele
Recipe Developer and Tester: Callie Nash
Assistant Production Manager: Diane Rose Keener
Assistant Production Director: Sue Chodakiewicz
Copy Editors: Julie Bosché, Ashley Strickland Freeman
Proofreaders: Rebecca Brennan, Julie Gillis
Indexer: Mary Ann Laurens
Fellow: Natalie Schumann

ISBN-13: 978-0-8487-4700-8
ISBN-10: 0-8487-4700-3
Library of Congress Control Number: 2015957930

First Edition 2016

Printed in the United States of America

10 9 8 7 6 5 4 3 2 1

Time Inc. Books products may be purchased for business or promotional use. For information on bulk purchases, please contact Christi Crowley in the Special Sales Department at (845) 895-9858.

We welcome your comments and suggestions about Time Inc. Books.
Please write to us at:
Time Inc. Books
Attention: Book Editors
P.O. Box 62310
Tampa, Florida 33662-2310

Southern Living

THE SOUTHERN
COOKIE
BOOK

Oxmoor
House®

CONTENTS

INTRODUCTION

The world loves cookies. The English have their biscuits, Germans enjoy keks, and Italians love to dunk biscotti or amaretti into whatever they might be sipping. While the affinity for cookies is universal, distinctions abound. The regional flavors, ingredients, and recipes of the South inspire the recipes in this book, so don't be surprised to find cornmeal mixed with the flour or a batter spiked with Kentucky bourbon. You'll also find cookie recipes inspired by classic Southern desserts like *Mississippi Mud Medallions* (page 275), *Hummingbird Oatmeal Cookies* (page 63), and *Red Velvet Brownies* (page 208). Whether you crave sweet or savory, round or square, dropped, rolled, or filled, you will find recipes for cookies, bars, brownies, and confections to suit every occasion and taste so no cookie jar is left unfilled. No matter where you live, or whether you are a seasoned baker or cookie rookie, you will appreciate the tried-and-tested tips and techniques for baking success brought to you by the South's most trusted kitchen at *Southern Living*.

Happy dunking,

Katherine Cobbs, Senior Editor

BATTER UP: GET INTO THE SWING WITH THESE BASIC TOOLS

Any way you roll, drop, or slice it, you need a few basic tools to cover your bases.

MIXING BOWLS

A set of metal or glass nesting bowls in three different sizes equals one for every task—mixing dry ingredients, creaming butter and sugar, or melting chocolate.

MEASURING CUPS AND SPOONS

A heavy-duty metal set of measuring cups for dry ingredients and glass measuring cups with a lip in sizes up to 4 quarts for liquids are workhorses of the baker's kitchen. A set of measuring spoons on a ring keeps things together and tidy.

WHISK

For beating eggs, whipping egg whites or cream, or whisking dry ingredients, a balloon whisk is a must.

SIFTER/MESH STRAINER

Whether you use a hand-crank sifter or a wire-mesh strainer, both produce light, fluffy lump-free flour that yields tender baked goods. They may also be used to dust baked goods with powdered sugar or cocoa.

WOODEN SPOONS

For mixing batters, there are few better (or less expensive) tools in the kitchen.

ROLLING PIN

Whether you choose one made of wood or marble, with handles or without, choose a heavy one so you don't have to press too hard as you roll the dough.

SCOOPS

Ice cream-style scoops come in many sizes to portion dough with precision, and the trigger action of the scoops keeps hands clean.

SPATULAS

Choose flexible rubber ones for folding in ingredients and scraping down bowls, metal varieties for transferring cookies to cooling racks, and small offset spatulas for icing or moving smaller cookies from pan to plate.

COOKIE CUTTERS

With options in every shape and size imaginable, this is where you have fun with rolled cookie dough.

PARCHMENT PAPER

Make cleanup a cinch by lining pans with parchment to keep baked goods from sticking.

SHEET PANS

Larger than most baking sheets, jelly-roll pans with rims are all you need for baking cookies. Other options include insulated and nonstick baking sheets.

KITCHEN TIMER

If you don't use a wristwatch, cell phone, or tablet to time your baking, an old-fashioned timer is a must.

COOLING RACK

Raised mesh racks allow air to circulate around cookies so that they cool evenly and quickly.

COOKIE TINS

The best thing since sliced bread is the airtight container. Decorative ones are great for giving, but any kind keeps cookies fresh longer.

CANDY THERMOMETER

These are designed to precisely measure high temperatures of foods, such as caramel. Buy one with a clip attachment so you don't have to hold it while you stir.

BATTER UP: GO MAJOR LEAGUE WITH EQUIPMENT EXTRAS

These kitchen additions take cookie baking from great to grand slam.

MIXER (STAND AND HAND)

A heavy-duty stand mixer allows for hands-off mixing, comes with a variety of attachments, and is great for making dough. Turn to the trusty hand mixer for a light-duty alternative.

FOOD PROCESSOR

This tool makes tedious tasks like chopping, slicing, and shredding a snap. Look for a machine with a large feed tube and sturdy, sharp blades.

PASTRY BAGS AND TIPS

For applying frosting, creating decorative flourishes, and piping egg whites for meringues, look for an array of tips and disposable bags for easy cleanup.

PASTRY CUTTER

Similar to a pizza cutter, but with a much smaller wheel, pastry cutters come with smooth or fluted edges for decorative scalloped cuts.

SHAKER/DREDGER

This handheld cup with a perforated top allows for a fine dusting of powdered sugar or cocoa on cookies before or after baking.

SQUIRT BOTTLES

Often used for condiments, plastic bottles with a narrow spout are great for piping hot caramel or chocolate and make decorating and cleanup a breeze.

SILICONE MAT

These handy baking mats take away the need for parchment, wax paper, oil, or grease for baking pans. They are safe to heat up to oven temperatures of 475°F.

CITRUS ZESTER

A fine rasp-style grater is a multipurpose tool for grating everything from ginger to nutmeg and makes fine, frilly shavings of zest for accenting baked goods.

SPICE GRINDER

A small electric spice or coffee bean grinder allows you to grind whole spices as needed. Whole spices have a longer shelf life than ground spices and can be ground to yield just what you need for a recipe.

CITRUS REAMER

When lots of fresh citrus juice is required for a recipe, a ribbed wooden or upright glass reamer allows you to extract the most juice with just a twist of the wrist.

HEAVY SAUCEPAN

Designed for melting sugar or candy-making, a heavy-duty saucepan is key. Stainless steel is both nonreactive and light enough inside to make it easy to gauge when sugar has reached caramel-colored perfection.

DOUBLE BOILER

Great for gently heating sauces or melting chocolate, a double boiler is worth the investment. You can improvise with a stainless steel mixing bowl set over a saucepan of simmering water.

MADELEINE PAN OR LADYFINGER PANS

There seems to be a pan for everything, and the options make baking fun. Nonstick madeleine and ladyfinger pans are two great ones to add to the baker's kitchen.

COOKIE MOLDS, PRESSES, AND STAMPS

Create detailed and intricately designed cookies with these specialty cookie-baking tools.

BATTER UP: KNOW YOUR INGREDIENTS

A well-stocked pantry lets you bake a batch when the mood strikes.

FLOUR

All-purpose wheat flour is commonly used for cookies as wheat gluten gives baked goods structure. The wheat germ in whole-wheat flour goes rancid quickly, so the flour is best kept sealed in a zip-top bag and chilled.

CORNSTARCH

This fine powdery starch is made from finely ground corn kernels and is used primarily as a thickening agent. It is often added to flour to lighten its texture, and it lasts indefinitely sealed in a cool, dry place.

OATS

Old-fashioned oats are made from rolling whole oat kernels or groats. The quick-cooking variety is made from flattening oat groat bits. Most recipes will state which variety to use. Avoid instant oats in cookies as they will affect cooking time and texture.

BAKING SODA AND BAKING POWDER

Baking soda is sodium bicarbonate, a single-acting alkaline ingredient used as a leavening agent. It is mixed with dry ingredients. Once wet ingredients are added—especially acidic ones—it reacts and releases carbon dioxide to create light, airy baked goods. Baking powder is a blend of baking soda and tartaric acid. It is a double-acting leavening agent that first reacts when combined with wet ingredients and then a second time with the heat of the oven. Check package expiration dates as both ingredients lose efficacy over time.

CREAM OF TARTAR

This refined byproduct of wine making is used to stabilize whipped egg whites and also acts as a leavening agent. It lasts indefinitely.

SPICES

Whole spices last twice as long as ground, so buy spices whole and grind them as needed. Sealed in a cool, dark place, whole spices last 2 to 3 years, while ground spices begin to lose their potency within a year or two.

SUGARS

Granulated sugar is all-purpose and used in an array of cooking methods. Superfine or castor sugar is pulverized granulated sugar that readily dissolves in liquid. Powdered sugar has been ground to a fine powder to dissolve almost instantly and is used for frostings and dusting cookies and brownies. Brown sugar is granulated sugar combined with molasses that comes in more delicately flavored light or intensely flavored dark varieties.

SYRUPS

Corn syrup, maple syrup, honey, molasses, or sorghum all impart sweetness to recipes. Store at room temperature, and they will last forever.

CREAM

Whipping cream (30% to 36% butterfat) and heavy cream (36% to 40% butterfat) are the skimmed creams that rise to the top of milk. Both can be whipped and mixed into batters.

HALF-AND-HALF

As the name suggests, this is half cream and half milk. It is used to add richness to batters. In a pinch, it can be made by mixing equal parts milk and cream.

MILK

Fresh whole or reduced-fat (2%) cow's milk works best for cookies, with no noticeable difference in results. Originally, buttermilk was the liquid drained from churned butter. Today, it gets its thick, tangy flavor from added cultures. Its acidity reacts with leavening agents to create light, tender cookies. Evaporated milk is canned, concentrated milk from which 60% of the water has been removed through heating and evaporation. It can be used as is in recipes or reconstituted with water as a substitute for fresh milk. Sweetened condensed milk is a shelf-stable canned cow's milk-and-sugar blend that has been reduced to a thick, syrupy-sweet mixture and is often used in desserts. Unused portions of canned milk should be refrigerated.

EGGS

Use very fresh, large grade A brown or white hen eggs unless a recipe calls for a different size. Eggs act as leaveners in recipes when their moisture evaporates during baking. The fat in the yolks helps emulsify batter and adds richness to baked cookies. Egg whites help stabilize the dough and provide structure.

OIL

Vegetable, canola, and corn oil are good bets for baking and have a high smoke point and neutral flavor. Avocado and coconut oils also have high smoke points, but they impart a distinctive flavor and major hit to your wallet. Other options to try include peanut oil, sunflower oil, and safflower oil.

BUTTER

Butter contains 80% milkfat and comes unsalted, salted, and whipped. Avoid whipped butter which has too much air incorporated to get an accurate measure for baking.

SHORTENING

Solid shortening is 100% vegetable fat with no water content. It gives tenderness to baked goods but lacks butter-rich flavor.

BATTER UP: ACCENTS FOR COOKIE— DECORATING HOME RUNS

Drizzles, dusts, and sprinkles, oh my! Elevate your baked goods to all-star status.

COCOA POWDER

This unsweetened, pure ground chocolate adds color and flavor. Natural cocoa is acidic but lightest in color and is most often used in recipes that call for baking soda, which neutralizes its sharpness. Dutch process cocoa has been alkalinized to reduce its acidity and is the variety most commonly used to dust baked goods and desserts.

ESPRESSO POWDER

Typically dissolved in hot liquid and paired with chocolate in cookies, brownies, and confections, dry espresso powder may also be mixed with superfine sugar and cinnamon and used as a flavorful garnishing dust.

LUSTER DUST AND SPRAY

This edible shimmering powder can be a mess to work with but creates elegant cookies. Find it in an array of shades, even pearlized finishes, in jars or spray cans. Powders are mixed with a drop or two of liquid and painted on cookies.

BARS, MORSELS, AND CHUNKS

Bars of milk chocolate, dark chocolate, or white chocolate can be melted for dipping and drizzling, chopped into chunks, or shaved into curls for frilly garnishes on brownies or bars. Whether incorporated into the dough or pressed on the surface of cookies prior to baking, morsels have moved beyond chocolate and butterscotch and come in a variety of flavors and sizes. Stock up on seasonally-inspired flavors too.

CANDIES

From candy bars and miniature cups to peppermints and jelly beans, store-bought candies can be used to add favorite flavors or delightful colors to your baked treats.

FOOD COLORING

It only takes a drop or two to tint icing, frosting, or dough. Be sure to mix thoroughly to avoid a marbled effect.

SPRINKLES GALORE

Sprinkles refer to a variety of confectionery accents. Jimmies are the tiny, oblong, opaque candy garnishes that top cookies and ice cream and are said to be named for the operator of the machine at the factory where they were created. Nonpareils refer to the poppyseed-sized round candy balls. Dragees are round, often metallic, candy-coated garnishes reminiscent of tiny ball bearings, while sugar pearls are their more refined cousins with a lustrous finish. Sanding sugars are translucent sugar crystals available coarse or fine that can be applied before or after baking. Roll balls of dough in the sugar before baking for a crackled effect. To adhere sprinkles to baked cookies, brush the cookies with egg wash, or frost them first.

ICINGS, FROSTINGS, AND GLAZES

If a cookie recipe you're making doesn't include an icing or glaze recipe, or you're in a pinch for time, purchased cookie icing, royal icing, frosting, or glazes in tubs or tubes are decent conveniences. Tubes are like a built-in piping bag with tip, which makes decorating with precision easy.

DRIED FRUIT AND NUTS

Dried or candied fruit add a colorful accent and interesting texture and flavor to baked goods, so stock up on your favorites and keep them stored in airtight containers at a steady temperature. Nuts have a high fat content that makes them go rancid fast, especially in the kitchen's fluctuating heat. Buy in bulk and in season, and keep them sealed in the pantry up to a month, or freeze up to a year.

EXTRACTS AND FLAVORINGS

Extracts are distilled volatile oils and flavor compounds of a particular ingredient—herb, spice, fruit, or nut—concentrated in a solution of alcohol. Flavorings are less potent and often blended in a liquid such as glycerin or oil. Imitation extracts or artificial flavorings are replications of a flavoring when it is either too expensive or difficult to extract from its natural state.

A BAKER'S DOZEN TIPS FOR COOKIE ROOKIES

1. Read through the recipe from start to finish before you begin, and assemble all ingredients so everything is at the ready.

2. Measure liquid ingredients in glass measuring cups. Solids should be spooned into metal or plastic dry measuring cups. Pack brown sugar firmly into dry measuring cups for accurate measurement.

3. Coat glass measuring cups with cooking spray for easy removal when measuring syrups. Coat knives or scissors lightly with flour before chopping candied fruits to avoid sticking.

4. Mix batters just until the flour is incorporated and ingredients combined to avoid overworking the dough which translates to tough cookies.

5. Use heavy aluminum baking sheets. Dark sheets absorb heat, causing cookies to get overly browned; nonstick baking sheets are OK if not too dark. Insulated baking sheets require extended baking time.

6. Lightly grease baking sheets only when the recipe specifies it; otherwise, cookies may spread too much while baking. Use vegetable cooking spray instead of butter or margarine, which can burn.

7. Roll buttery dough on wax paper for a nonstick surface. When dough gets too soft, pop it in the fridge for 5 to 10 minutes to firm up.

8. Bake one batch of cookies at a time on the middle oven rack. If you must bake two, rotate pans from top to bottom halfway through baking to ensure even browning and doneness.

9. Always preheat the oven and bake with precision. For soft and chewy cookies, remove from the oven at the lower range of time. For crisper cookies, leave them in a minute or two longer.

10. Remove cookies from baking sheets when the recipe specifies. Transfer to a wire rack to cool. Do not stack them or let the sides touch while they are still warm. Cookies firm up as they cool.

11. Store soft, chewy cookies in an airtight container and crisp cookies in a container with a loose-fitting lid. Store bar cookies in their baking pan; seal the top of the pan with aluminum foil. Unfrosted bar cookies can be stacked and stored in airtight containers.

12. Unfrosted cookies freeze well for 8 months in zip-top plastic freezer bags, metal tins, or plastic freezer containers. Dough can be sealed and frozen up to 6 months. Thaw dough in the refrigerator or at room temperature until it's the right consistency for shaping.

13. Baking up a bake sale batch? Bag them up in style, but be sure to include a list of ingredients for those who may have food sensitivities or allergies.

DROP COOKIES

THE SCOOP ON PERFECT DROP COOKIES

Follow these simple steps to ensure drop cookies come out of the oven perfectly for bakery-worthy results every time.

1. Swap the spoon for a small scoop for perfectly portioned dough and clean hands too.

2. Arrange uniform scoops in rows with room between each, so baked cookies remain separate but equal.

3. Chill portioned dough to keep it from spreading as it bakes, and never drop a second batch on a hot cookie sheet.

4. When baking multiple batches, rotate cookie sheets halfway through baking for even browning.

5. Cookies are too soft to handle right from the oven. Transfer to a wire rack to cool when recipe specifies.

6. Baked drop cookies are great for frosting, sandwiching ice cream, or dunking in milk.

LEMON MELTAWAYS

HANDS-ON 30 MIN. TOTAL 2 HOURS

These heavenly treats conjure memories of summertime, like lemonade-stand refreshment in bite-size form.

1. Beat butter at medium speed with a heavy-duty electric stand mixer until creamy. Add ½ cup powdered sugar; beat at medium speed until light and fluffy. Stir in zest and juice. Whisk together flour and next 2 ingredients. Gradually add flour mixture to butter mixture, beating at low speed just until blended. Cover and chill 1 hour.

2. Preheat oven to 350°F. Drop dough by level spoonfuls 2 inches apart onto parchment paper-lined baking sheets, using a 1-inch cookie scoop.

3. Bake, in batches, at 350°F for 13 minutes or until lightly browned around edges. Cool on baking sheets 5 minutes.

4. Toss together warm cookies and remaining 1 cup powdered sugar in a small bowl. Transfer to wire racks, and cool completely (about 15 minutes).

MAKES about 3½ dozen

⭐ PARTY PERFECT

These sugar-dusted beauties are as pretty arranged on a tray for a springtime baby shower as they are piled in a pyramid on a cake stand for a snowy cookie tree at Christmas.

INGREDIENTS

¾ cup plus 2 Tbsp. butter, softened

1½ cups powdered sugar, divided

1 Tbsp. loosely packed lemon zest

2 Tbsp. fresh lemon juice

1½ cups all-purpose flour

¼ cup cornstarch

¼ tsp. table salt

Parchment paper

HONEY-HAZELNUT CRISPS

INGREDIENTS

¾ cup powdered sugar

½ cup butter, softened

1 Tbsp. honey

¼ tsp. vanilla extract

⅛ tsp. kosher salt

½ cup finely chopped hazelnuts

6 Tbsp. all-purpose flour

3 Tbsp. whole wheat flour

Parchment paper

HANDS-ON 15 MIN. TOTAL 1 HOUR, 30 MIN.

These lacy cookies keep best in a tin between sheets of wax paper. Use tupelo or buckwheat honey for a touch of Southern sweetness.

1. Preheat oven to 325°F. Beat first 5 ingredients at medium speed with an electric mixer 4 to 5 minutes or until creamy. Add hazelnuts and next 2 ingredients; beat just until blended.

2. Drop dough by level teaspoonfuls 3 inches apart onto 2 parchment paper-lined baking sheets.

3. Bake, in batches, at 325°F for 12 to 14 minutes or until golden brown around edges. Cool on baking sheets 5 minutes. Transfer to wire racks, and cool completely (about 30 minutes).

MAKES about 4½ dozen

COOKIE SWAP

For Hazelnut Fig Sandwiches, prepare as directed. Spoon ½ cup fig preserves on half of cookies (about 1 tsp. per cookie); top with remaining cookies. Makes about 2 dozen.

MISSISSIPPI PRALINE MACAROONS

Hands-on 20 min. Total 1 hour, 20 min.

The classic version of this airy cookie originated in Italy, but toasted pecans stand in for the traditional almonds here, giving this macaroon recipe a decidedly Southern twist.

1. Preheat oven to 325°F. Beat egg whites, cream of tartar, and salt at high speed with a heavy-duty electric stand mixer using whisk attachment, until foamy; gradually add brown sugar, beating until stiff peaks form and sugar dissolves. Gently fold in toasted chopped pecans.

2. Drop batter by heaping teaspoonfuls 1 inch apart onto lightly greased (with cooking spray) aluminum foil-lined baking sheets. Press 1 pecan half into each cookie, flattening slightly.

3. Bake, in batches, at 325°F for 33 minutes or until pecan halves are toasted and cookies are lightly browned. Cool on baking sheets 1 minute; transfer to wire racks, and let cool 20 minutes. (Cookies will crisp while cooling.) Store in airtight containers up to 1 week.

MAKES about 3 dozen

SMART COOKIE

Don't leave out the small amount of cream of tartar called for in this recipe. It acts as a stabilizer for the egg whites, increasing their volume and heat tolerance and thus the praise you'll get when serving these delicate treats.

INGREDIENTS

3 large egg whites, at room temperature

¼ tsp. cream of tartar

Pinch of table salt

1 cup firmly packed light brown sugar

1 cup toasted coarsely chopped pecans

Vegetable cooking spray

36 pecan halves

TOASTED COCONUT COOKIES

INGREDIENTS

¼ cup butter, softened

¼ cup shortening

1 cup sugar

1 large egg

½ tsp. coconut extract

1½ cups all-purpose
flour

1 tsp. baking powder

½ tsp. baking soda

½ tsp. table salt

1 cup sweetened
flaked coconut

½ cup crispy rice cereal

½ cup uncooked
regular oats

Vegetable cooking spray

HANDS-ON 20 MIN. TOTAL 1 HOUR, 15 MIN.

The distinctive flavor of coconut is beloved in the South—from ambrosia to coconut cream pie and coconut layer cake—and this cookie is one for the recipe box.

1. Preheat oven to 325°F. Beat butter and shortening at medium speed with an electric mixer until creamy; gradually add sugar, beating until blended. Add egg and coconut extract, beating until blended.

2. Combine flour, baking powder, baking soda, and salt in a small bowl; gradually add flour mixture to butter mixture, beating until blended after each addition. Stir in coconut, cereal, and oats.

3. Drop dough by heaping teaspoonfuls onto lightly greased (with cooking spray) baking sheets.

4. Bake, in batches, at 325°F for 12 to 14 minutes or until golden brown. Cool on baking sheets 5 minutes. Transfer to wire racks, and cool completely (about 20 minutes).

MAKES 4 dozen

WHITE CHOCOLATE-ORANGE DREAM COOKIES

Hands-on 15 min. Total 1 hour, 5 min.

If fresh Southern-grown satsumas, the small mandarin oranges with a fragrant zest and sweet juice, are in season and available in your area, seek them out for this recipe.

1. Preheat oven to 350°F. Beat first 3 ingredients at medium speed with an electric mixer until creamy. Add egg, orange zest, and orange extract, beating until blended.

2. Combine flour, baking soda, and salt in a small bowl; gradually add flour mixture to butter mixture, beating until just blended after each addition. Stir in white chocolate morsels.

3. Drop dough by rounded tablespoonfuls onto ungreased baking sheets.

4. Bake, in batches, at 350°F for 10 to 12 minutes or until lightly browned around edges. Cool on baking sheets 2 minutes. Transfer to wire racks, and cool completely (about 20 minutes).

MAKES about 3½ dozen

INGREDIENTS

1 cup butter, softened

⅔ cup firmly packed light brown sugar

½ cup granulated sugar

1 large egg

1 Tbsp. loosely packed orange zest

2 tsp. orange extract

2¼ cups all-purpose flour

¾ tsp. baking soda

½ tsp. table salt

2 cups white chocolate morsels

TROPICAL WHITE CHOCOLATE COOKIES

¾ cup butter, softened

¾ cup firmly packed brown sugar

¾ cup granulated sugar

1 tsp. vanilla extract

2 large eggs

1½ cups sweetened flaked coconut

1 Tbsp. loosely packed lime zest

2 Tbsp. fresh lime juice

2½ cups all-purpose flour

1 tsp. baking soda

½ tsp. table salt

1 (12-oz.) package white chocolate morsels

½ cup chopped macadamia nuts

Hands-on 15 min. Total 50 min.

White chocolate has a rich, neutral flavor that lets the brightness of citrus shine. For authentic flavor from Key West, substitute Key lime zest and juice when available.

1. Preheat oven to 375°F. Beat first 4 ingredients at medium speed with an electric mixer until creamy. Add eggs, beating until blended. Add coconut, lime zest, and lime juice, beating until blended.

2. Combine flour, baking soda, and salt in a small bowl; gradually add flour mixture to butter mixture, beating until blended. Stir in white chocolate morsels and macadamia nuts.

3. Drop dough by rounded tablespoonfuls onto ungreased baking sheets.

4. Bake, in batches, at 375°F for 10 to 12 minutes or until lightly browned. Transfer to wire racks, and cool completely (about 20 minutes).

MAKES about 4 dozen

COOKIE SWAP

For a refreshing island twist, spoon ¼ to ½ cup lime sherbet between two cookies. Seal in plastic wrap, and freeze until ready to serve.

SOUTHERN ROCKS

Hands-on 20 min. Total 1 hour, 30 min.

These fruitcake-inspired sweets are so loaded with dried fruits and nuts that they come out of the oven looking like boulders of goodness. This recipe calls for brushing the finished cookies with Kentucky bourbon instead of the traditional brandy.

1. Preheat oven to 325°F. Beat brown sugar and butter at medium speed with an electric mixer until smooth. Add eggs, beating until blended.

2. Combine flour and next 5 ingredients in a medium bowl; gradually add flour mixture to butter mixture, beating until blended. Add bourbon, beating until blended.

3. Combine pecans and next 4 ingredients in a large bowl. Pour batter over pecan mixture, and stir until blended.

4. Drop dough by rounded teaspoonfuls 2 inches apart onto lightly greased (with cooking spray) baking sheets.

5. Bake, in batches, at 325°F for 20 minutes or until lightly browned. Remove from oven, and immediately brush with bourbon, if desired. Cool on baking sheets 2 to 3 minutes. Transfer to wire racks, and cool completely (about 30 minutes).

MAKES 4 dozen

⭐ PARTY PERFECT

Package these rather retro treats to give as host or hostess gifts during the holidays. Look for vintage tins or cookie jars for two gifts in one.

INGREDIENTS

¾ cup firmly packed light brown sugar

½ cup butter, softened

2 large eggs

1½ cups all-purpose flour

1 tsp. ground cinnamon

½ tsp. baking soda

¼ tsp. table salt

¼ tsp. ground cloves

¼ tsp. ground allspice

¼ cup bourbon or apple juice

2 cups chopped pecans

½ lb. candied cherries, halved

½ lb. candied pineapple, chopped

1 cup pitted dates, chopped

1 cup raisins

Vegetable cooking spray

2 to 3 Tbsp. bourbon (optional)

SMOKY MOUNTAIN SNOWCAPS

INGREDIENTS

1 (6-oz.) white chocolate baking bar, chopped

¾ cup butter, softened

1 cup granulated sugar

3 large eggs

1 tsp. vanilla extract

3½ cups all-purpose flour

1 tsp. baking powder

¾ tsp. table salt

⅛ tsp. ground nutmeg

1½ cups toasted chopped walnuts or pecans

Parchment paper

½ cup powdered sugar

HANDS-ON 15 MIN. TOTAL 1 HOUR, 5 MIN.

A few snowflakes are a rarity throughout much of the South, but the highest peaks of Tennessee's Smoky Mountains average more than 5½ feet of snow each winter. The little mountains of goodness inside these delicious treats get a dusting of powdered sugar that's as sweet as a snowy day. They freeze well too.

1. Preheat oven to 350°F. Melt white chocolate in a small saucepan over low heat, stirring until melted and smooth.

2. Beat butter and granulated sugar at medium speed with an electric mixer 5 minutes or until fluffy. Add eggs, 1 at a time, beating until blended after each addition. Add vanilla, beating until blended. Add melted chocolate, and beat 30 seconds.

3. Combine flour and next 3 ingredients in a medium bowl; add flour mixture to butter mixture, beating until blended. Stir in walnuts.

4. Drop dough by heaping tablespoonfuls onto parchment paper-lined baking sheets.

5. Bake, in batches, at 350°F for 10 to 12 minutes or until lightly browned around edges. Transfer to wire racks, and cool completely (about 30 minutes). Sprinkle with powdered sugar.

MAKES 3½ dozen

CHAI TEA EGGNOG COOKIES

Hands-on 20 min. Total 45 min.

While chai tea may seem more Far East than Deep South, Southerners do have an affinity for tea, especially the sweet kind. Mix in a little bourbon-spiked eggnog, and you've got a cookie that will make pretty much any sweet tooth happy.

1. Preheat oven to 350°F. Remove tea leaves from tea bag; discard bag.

2. Combine tea leaves, cookie mix, butter, egg, and 2 Tbsp. eggnog in a medium bowl, beating until blended.

3. Drop dough by tablespoonfuls onto parchment paper-lined baking sheets. Flatten dough slightly with bottom of a glass dipped in cinnamon-sugar.

4. Bake, in batches, at 350°F for 8 to 10 minutes or until lightly browned. Transfer to wire racks, and cool completely (about 10 minutes).

5. Whisk together powdered sugar, nutmeg, and remaining 2 Tbsp. eggnog until smooth; spoon over cooled cookies.

MAKES 2 dozen

SMART COOKIE

What sets chai tea apart from the leaves we brew for sweet tea in the South? Only the addition of a few warm spices like cardamom, cinnamon, fennel seed, cloves, and star anise—all delicious additions to cookies and other baked goods.

INGREDIENTS

1 chai tea bag

1 (17.5-oz.) package sugar cookie mix

½ cup butter, melted

1 large egg

4 Tbsp. eggnog, divided

Parchment paper

Cinnamon-sugar

1 cup powdered sugar

½ tsp. freshly grated nutmeg

ALMOND-TOFFEE COOKIES

INGREDIENTS

¾ cup butter, softened

¾ cup granulated sugar

¾ cup firmly packed dark brown sugar

2 large eggs

1½ tsp. vanilla extract

2¼ cups plus 2 Tbsp. all-purpose flour

1 tsp. baking soda

¾ tsp. table salt

6 (1.4-oz.) chopped chocolate-covered toffee candy bars

1½ cups toasted slivered almonds

Parchment paper

½ cup semisweet chocolate morsels

Hands-on 30 min. Total 1 hour

Crunchy and sweet with a buttery finish, toffee elevates this cookie to star status. Seek out Southern toffee like Almond Toffee Crumbles from the Nashville Toffee Company. Bake 10 minutes for a soft and chewy cookie or up to 14 minutes for a crisp cookie.

1. Preheat oven to 350°F. Beat butter and sugars at medium speed with a heavy-duty electric stand mixer until creamy. Add eggs and vanilla, beating until blended.

2. Combine flour, baking soda, and salt in a small bowl; gradually add flour mixture to butter mixture, beating just until blended. Beat in chopped toffee candy bars and slivered almonds just until combined.

3. Drop dough by tablespoonfuls onto parchment paper-lined baking sheets.

4. Bake, in batches, at 350°F for 10 to 14 minutes or until desired degree of doneness. Transfer to wire racks, and cool completely (about 15 minutes).

5. Microwave chocolate morsels in a small microwave-safe bowl at HIGH 1 minute or until melted and smooth, stirring after 30 seconds. Spoon chocolate into a small zip-top plastic freezer bag; seal bag. Snip 1 corner of bag to make a tiny hole. Drizzle a small amount of chocolate over each cookie.

MAKES about 5 dozen

OUTRAGEOUS PEANUT BUTTER COOKIES

Hands-on 10 min. Total 40 min.

The fully loaded candy bar takes this small-batch cookie from great to over the top! Feel free to substitute your favorite candy bar.

1. Preheat oven to 325°F. Combine flour and baking soda in a small bowl.

2. Beat brown sugar and next 3 ingredients at low speed with an electric mixer 1 minute or until blended. Add peanut butter, and beat 20 seconds or until blended. Add flour mixture; beat 30 seconds or until well blended. Stir in oats and chopped candy bar.

3. Drop dough by heaping tablespoonfuls 2 inches apart onto a parchment paper-lined baking sheet. Flatten dough slightly with bottom of a glass dipped in granulated sugar.

4. Bake at 325°F for 15 to 20 minutes or until lightly browned. Cool on baking sheet 2 minutes. Transfer to wire rack, and cool completely (about 15 minutes).

*2 tsp. egg substitute may be substituted for beaten egg.

NOTE: We used Reese's NutRageous candy bar, but use your favorite.

MAKES 8 cookies

COOKIE SWAP

For Outrageous Peanut Butter-and-Jelly Cookies, spread 1 to 2 tsp. of your favorite jam or jelly onto cooled cookies.

INGREDIENTS

¼ cup all-purpose flour

⅛ tsp. baking soda

¼ cup firmly packed dark brown sugar

2 Tbsp. butter, softened

2 tsp. well-beaten egg*

¼ tsp. vanilla extract

⅓ cup extra-chunky peanut butter

1½ Tbsp. uncooked regular oats

½ (1.8-oz.) chocolate-coated caramel-peanut butter-peanut candy bar, chopped

Parchment paper

1 Tbsp. granulated sugar

BROWNIE COOKIES

Could a cookie have an identity problem? Well, one bite of this double chocolate cookie will remind you of a thick and fudgy brownie. Indulge!

INGREDIENTS

½ cup butter

4 (1-oz.) unsweetened chocolate baking squares, chopped

3 cups semisweet chocolate morsels, divided

1½ cups all-purpose flour

½ tsp. baking powder

½ tsp. table salt

4 large eggs

1½ cups sugar

2 tsp. vanilla extract

2 cups toasted chopped pecans

Parchment paper

1. Preheat oven to 350°F. Combine butter, unsweetened chocolate, and 1½ cups chocolate morsels in a large heavy saucepan over low heat, and cook, stirring constantly, until butter and chocolate are melted; cool.

2. Combine flour, baking powder, and salt in a small bowl; set aside.

3. Beat eggs, sugar, and vanilla at medium speed with an electric mixer until combined; gradually add flour mixture to egg mixture, beating until blended. Add chocolate mixture; beat until blended. Stir in remaining 1½ cups chocolate morsels and pecans.

4. Drop dough by 2 tablespoonfuls 1 inch apart onto parchment paper-lined baking sheets.

5. Bake, in batches, at 350°F for 10 minutes. Cool on baking sheets 5 minutes. Transfer to wire racks, and cool completely (about 20 minutes).

MAKES 2½ dozen

CHOCOLATE-DIPPED TOFFEE-PECAN COOKIES

HANDS-ON 30 MIN. TOTAL 2 HOURS

These are over-the-top decadent with pecans, toffee, and chocolate nestled into the cookies as well as sprinkled on top. If you don't want to make all of the cookies at once, refrigerate the dough in an airtight container for up to one week.

1. Preheat oven to 375°F. Beat butter at medium speed with an electric mixer until creamy; gradually add sugars, beating until light and fluffy (about 3 minutes). Add egg and vanilla; beat until blended.

2. Combine flour, baking soda, and salt in a medium bowl; gradually add flour mixture to butter mixture, beating at low speed just until blended after each addition. Stir in 1 cup pecans, toffee bars, and 2 chopped chocolate baking bars.

3. Drop dough by heaping tablespoonfuls 2 inches apart onto parchment paper-lined baking sheets.

4. Bake, in batches, at 375°F for 11 to 13 minutes or until golden brown. Cool on baking sheets 5 minutes. Transfer to wire racks, and cool completely (about 30 minutes).

5. Microwave remaining 2 chopped chocolate bars at HIGH 1½ minutes or until melted, stirring every 30 seconds. Dip half of the top of each cookie into melted chocolate, letting excess drip off. Place on parchment paper-lined baking sheets. Sprinkle with remaining pecans and sea salt. Let stand 30 minutes or until set.

MAKES about 3 dozen

INGREDIENTS

1 cup butter, softened

1 cup firmly packed light brown sugar

½ cup granulated sugar

1 large egg

2 tsp. vanilla extract

2½ cups all-purpose flour

¾ tsp. baking soda

¼ tsp. table salt

1½ cups toasted chopped pecans, divided

3 (1.4-oz.) chocolate-covered toffee candy bars, chopped

4 (4-oz.) bittersweet chocolate baking bars, chopped, divided

Parchment paper

Flaky sea salt

ULTIMATE CHOCOLATE CHIP COOKIES

HANDS-ON 30 MIN. TOTAL 1 HOUR, 15 MIN.

These classic chocolate chip cookies are sure to be an instant hit with family and friends. A heap of dark brown sugar adds rich flavor to the dough.

1. Preheat oven to 350°F. Beat butter and sugars at medium speed with an electric mixer until creamy. Add eggs and vanilla, beating until blended.

2. Combine flour, baking soda, and salt in a small bowl; gradually add flour mixture to butter mixture, beating until blended. Stir in chocolate morsels.

3. Drop dough by tablespoonfuls onto lightly greased (with cooking spray) baking sheets.

4. Bake, in batches, at 350°F for 8 to 14 minutes or until desired degree of doneness. Transfer to wire racks, and cool completely (about 20 minutes).

MAKES about 5 dozen

COOKIE SWAP

For a new spin every time you bake, change up the flavor of the morsels you use from chocolate to butterscotch, peanut butter, or even mint- or cherry-filled varieties.

INGREDIENTS

¾ cup butter, softened

¾ cup granulated sugar

¾ cup firmly packed dark brown sugar

2 large eggs

1½ tsp. vanilla extract

2¼ cups plus 2 Tbsp. all-purpose flour

1 tsp. baking soda

¾ tsp. table salt

1 (12-oz.) package semisweet chocolate morsels

Vegetable cooking spray

CHUNKY CHOCOLATE GOBS

Hands-on 20 min. Total 1 hour, 40 min.

These gobs of goodness are, hands down, some of the best ever to come through our Test Kitchen.

1. Preheat oven to 350°F. Beat butter and shortening at medium speed with an electric mixer until creamy; gradually add sugars, beating until fluffy. Add eggs and vanilla, beating until blended.

2. Combine flour and next 3 ingredients in a medium bowl; gradually add flour mixture to butter mixture, beating until blended. Stir in sandwich cookies, candy bars, and desired amount of chocolate morsels. Chill dough 30 minutes.

3. Drop dough by ¼ cupfuls 2 inches apart onto parchment paper-lined baking sheets.

4. Bake, in batches, at 350°F for 10 to 12 minutes or until barely set. Cool on baking sheets 10 minutes. Transfer to wire racks, and cool completely (about 20 minutes).

MAKES about 2½ dozen

SMART COOKIE

Toss old cans of shortening for your health. All shortening sold today must be free of trans fats, thanks to a ruling by the USDA. Look for all-natural varieties too.

INGREDIENTS

¾ cup unsalted butter, softened

⅓ cup butter-flavored shortening

1 cup granulated sugar

⅔ cup firmly packed dark brown sugar

2 large eggs

2 tsp. vanilla extract

2 cups all-purpose flour

⅔ cup unsweetened cocoa

1 tsp. baking soda

¼ tsp. table salt

2 cups cream-filled chocolate sandwich cookies, coarsely chopped (16 cookies)

3 (1.75-oz.) dark-chocolate-covered coconut candy bars, chilled and chopped

1 to 2 cups semisweet chocolate morsels

Parchment paper

CHOCOLATE CHUNK-MOCHA COOKIES

INGREDIENTS

1 cup butter, softened

¾ cup granulated sugar

⅔ cup firmly packed brown sugar

1 tsp. vanilla extract

2 large eggs

2¼ cups all-purpose flour

⅔ cup unsweetened cocoa

1 tsp. baking soda

¼ tsp. table salt

1 (11.5-oz.) package semisweet chocolate chunks

Parchment paper

Mocha Frosting

Powdered sugar (optional)

HANDS-ON 25 MIN. TOTAL 1 HOUR, 10 MIN.

Filled with chunks of chocolate and covered in Mocha Frosting, these delicious drop cookies received our Test Kitchen's highest rating.

1. Preheat oven to 350°F. Beat butter and next 3 ingredients at medium speed with an electric mixer until creamy. Add eggs, 1 at a time, beating just until blended after each addition.

2. Combine flour and next 3 ingredients in a medium bowl; gradually add flour mixture to butter mixture, beating at low speed until blended. Stir in chocolate chunks.

3. Drop dough by heaping tablespoonfuls onto parchment paper-lined baking sheets.

4. Bake, in batches, at 350°F for 10 to 12 minutes or until puffy. Cool on baking sheets 2 minutes. Transfer to wire racks, and cool completely (about 30 minutes). Spread cookies with Mocha Frosting. Sprinkle evenly with powdered sugar, if desired.

MAKES 3 dozen

MOCHA FROSTING

Stir together **¼ cup unsweetened cocoa, ¼ cup hot strong brewed coffee, ¼ cup melted butter,** and **1 tsp. vanilla extract** until smooth. Gradually stir in **3½ cups sifted powdered sugar** until creamy.

CHUNKY CHERRY-DOUBLE CHIP COOKIES

Hands-on 30 min. Total 1 hour, 25 min.

Cherries, white and dark chocolate, and a handful of toasted almonds take these easy drop cookies to heavenly heights.

1. Preheat oven to 350°F. Microwave 1 Tbsp. water and dried cherries in a glass bowl at HIGH 30 seconds, stirring once. Let stand 10 minutes.

2. Beat butter and sugars at medium speed with an electric mixer until creamy. Add eggs and vanilla, beating until blended.

3. Combine flour, baking soda, and salt in a small bowl; gradually add flour mixture to butter mixture, beating until blended. Stir in semisweet chocolate chunks, white chocolate morsels, almonds, and cherries.

4. Drop dough by tablespoonfuls onto lightly greased (with cooking spray) baking sheets.

5. Bake, in batches, at 350°F for 8 to 14 minutes or until desired degree of doneness. Transfer to wire racks, and cool completely (about 20 minutes).

MAKES about 5 dozen

INGREDIENTS

½ cup dried cherries

¾ cup butter, softened

¾ cup granulated sugar

¾ cup firmly packed dark brown sugar

2 large eggs

1½ tsp. vanilla extract

2¼ cups plus 2 Tbsp. all-purpose flour

1 tsp. baking soda

¾ tsp. table salt

1 (12-oz.) package semisweet chocolate chunks

1 cup white chocolate morsels

⅓ cup slivered toasted almonds

Vegetable cooking spray

INGREDIENTS

6 (1-oz.) semisweet chocolate baking squares, chopped

2 (1-oz.) unsweetened chocolate squares, chopped

⅓ cup butter

3 large eggs

1 cup sugar

¼ cup all-purpose flour

½ tsp. baking powder

⅛ tsp. table salt

2 cups (12 oz.) semisweet chocolate morsels

2 cups coarsely chopped pecans

2 cups coarsely chopped walnuts

CHOCOLATE CHUBBIES

HANDS-ON 15 MIN. TOTAL 1 HOUR

How can you go wrong with this much chocolate packed into one fat cookie? And chances are you already have most of the ingredients on hand.

1. Preheat oven to 325°F. Combine first 3 ingredients in a heavy saucepan over low heat, and cook, stirring often, until chocolate is melted. Remove from heat; cool slightly.

2. Beat eggs and sugar at medium speed with an electric mixer until smooth; add chocolate mixture, beating until blended.

3. Combine flour, baking powder, and salt in a small bowl; add flour mixture to chocolate mixture, stirring just until dry ingredients are moistened. Fold in chocolate morsels, pecans, and walnuts.

4. Drop batter by tablespoonfuls 2 inches apart onto lightly greased baking sheets.

5. Bake, in batches, at 325°F for 12 to 15 minutes or until almost set. Cool on baking sheets, 1 minute. Transfer to wire racks, and cool completely (about 20 minutes).

MAKES 3½ dozen

OATMEAL, GOLDEN RAISIN, AND BUTTERSCOTCH DROPS

Hands-on 10 min. Total 1 hour

Put a newfangled spin on a batch of old-fashioned oatmeal cookies by adding butterscotch chips and golden raisins.

1. Preheat oven to 350°F. Beat butter and sugars at medium speed with an electric mixer until creamy. Add eggs and vanilla, beating until blended.

2. Combine flour, baking soda, oats, and salt in a small bowl; gradually add flour mixture to butter mixture, beating until blended. Stir in butterscotch morsels and raisins.

3. Drop dough by tablespoonfuls onto lightly greased (with cooking spray) baking sheets.

4. Bake, in batches, at 350°F for 8 to 14 minutes or until desired degree of doneness. Transfer to wire racks, and cool completely (about 15 minutes).

MAKES about 5 dozen

INGREDIENTS

¾ cup butter, softened

¾ cup granulated sugar

¾ cup firmly packed dark brown sugar

2 large eggs

1½ tsp. vanilla extract

2 cups all-purpose flour

1 tsp. baking soda

1 cup uncooked quick-cooking oats

¾ tsp. table salt

1 (12-oz.) package butterscotch morsels

1 cup golden raisins

Vegetable cooking spray

OATMEAL-PECAN SNACK COOKIES

INGREDIENTS

¼ cup butter, softened

6 oz. reduced-fat cream cheese, softened

1½ cups firmly packed dark brown sugar

½ cup egg substitute

1 tsp. vanilla extract

1¾ cups all-purpose flour

1¾ tsp. pumpkin pie spice

½ tsp. table salt

½ tsp. baking soda

3 cups uncooked regular oats

¾ cup dried cherries

Vegetable cooking spray

½ cup chopped pecans

Hands-on 20 min. Total 1 hour

Try these nutritious cookies, studded with Southern pecans, with a glass of cold milk for breakfast on the go.

1. Preheat oven to 350°F. Beat butter, cream cheese, and brown sugar at medium speed with an electric mixer until fluffy. Add egg substitute and vanilla, beating until blended.

2. Combine flour, pumpkin pie spice, salt, and baking soda in a medium bowl; gradually add flour mixture to butter mixture, beating at low speed just until blended. Stir in oats and dried cherries.

3. Drop dough by rounded tablespoonfuls onto lightly greased (with cooking spray) baking sheets. Gently flatten dough into circles. Sprinkle about ½ tsp. chopped pecans onto each dough circle, gently pressing into dough.

4. Bake, in batches, at 350°F for 13 to 14 minutes or until a wooden pick inserted in centers comes out clean. Transfer to wire racks, and cool 10 minutes.

MAKES about 4 dozen

COOKIE SWAP

For Carrot-Oatmeal-Pecan Snack Cookies, prepare dough as directed through Step 2, stirring in 2 grated carrots with oats and cherries. Proceed with recipe as directed.

HUMMINGBIRD OATMEAL COOKIES

Hands-on 30 min. Total 1 hour, 40 min.

These cookies are inspired by the famous Hummingbird Cake recipe submitted by Mrs. L.H. Wiggins of North Carolina, featured in the February 1978 issue of Southern Living. *No time for frosting? They're delicious unadorned, too.*

1. Preheat oven to 350°F. Beat butter, brown sugar, and vanilla at medium speed with an electric mixer 3 to 5 minutes or until creamy. Add eggs, 1 at a time, beating until blended after each addition.

2. Combine flour, cinnamon, baking soda, and salt in a medium bowl; gradually add flour mixture and mashed banana to butter mixture, beating just until blended. Add oats and next 2 ingredients; stir until blended.

3. Drop dough by heaping tablespoonfuls 2 inches apart onto 2 parchment paper-lined baking sheets. Flatten dough slightly with bottom of a glass dipped in flour.

4. Bake, in batches, at 350°F for 12 minutes or until golden. Cool on baking sheets 10 minutes. Transfer to wire racks, and cool completely (about 20 minutes).

5. Spread Cream Cheese Frosting over each cookie (about 1½ tsp. per cookie); sprinkle with banana chips, coconut, and toasted chopped pecans, pressing to adhere.

MAKES 4 dozen

CREAM CHEESE FROSTING

Beat **2 cups sifted powdered sugar, 4 oz. softened cream cheese, 1 tsp. vanilla extract,** and **½ tsp. kosher salt** with an electric mixer 3 to 5 minutes or until creamy. Add **¼ cup heavy cream,** and beat until smooth.

INGREDIENTS

1 cup butter, softened

1 cup firmly packed light brown sugar

1 tsp. vanilla extract

2 large eggs

2 cups all-purpose flour

2 tsp. ground cinnamon

1 tsp. baking soda

½ tsp. kosher salt

½ medium-size ripe banana, mashed

1½ cups uncooked regular oats

1 cup finely chopped pecans

½ cup finely chopped dried pineapple

Parchment paper

Cream Cheese Frosting

½ cup chopped dried banana chips

½ cup sweetened flaked coconut, toasted

½ cup toasted chopped pecans

CRISPY PRALINE COOKIES

HANDS-ON 4 MIN. TOTAL 35 MIN.

This cookie rendition of the classic Southern praline swaps chocolate for the nuts, and the result is a magical mouthful.

1. Preheat oven to 350°F. Combine all ingredients in a large bowl, stirring until blended.

2. Drop dough by tablespoonfuls onto ungreased baking sheets.

3. Bake, in batches, at 350°F for 13 to 15 minutes. Cool on baking sheets 1 minute. Transfer to wire rack, and cool completely (about 15 minutes).

MAKES about 2 dozen

INGREDIENTS

1 cup all-purpose flour

1 cup firmly packed
dark brown sugar

1 large egg

½ cup butter, softened

1 tsp. vanilla extract

1 cup semisweet
chocolate morsels

SMART COOKIE

The French brought crunchy pralines—a mixture of almonds and caramelized sugar—to Louisiana. Over time, they evolved into a softer, creamier confection made with Southern-grown pecans.

CHOCOLATE CHIP PRETZEL COOKIES

Hands-on 30 min. Total 1 hour, 15 min.

A good Southerner never arrives (or lets guests leave) empty-handed. This salty-sweet variation on the classic chocolate chip cookie will win over anyone. Bake 10 minutes for a soft and chewy cookie or up to 14 minutes for a crisp cookie.

1. Preheat oven to 350°F. Beat butter and sugars at medium speed with a heavy-duty electric stand mixer until creamy. Add eggs and vanilla, beating until blended.

2. Combine flour, baking soda, and salt in a small bowl; gradually add flour mixture to butter mixture, beating just until blended. Beat in chocolate morsels and pretzel sticks just until combined.

3. Drop dough by tablespoonfuls onto parchment paper-lined baking sheets.

4. Bake, in batches, at 350°F for 10 to 14 minutes or until desired degree of doneness. Transfer to wire racks, and cool completely (about 15 minutes).

MAKES about 5 dozen

INGREDIENTS

¾ cup butter, softened

¾ cup granulated sugar

¾ cup firmly packed dark brown sugar

2 large eggs

1½ tsp. vanilla extract

2¼ cups plus 2 Tbsp. all-purpose flour

1 tsp. baking soda

¾ tsp. table salt

1½ (12-oz.) packages semisweet chocolate morsels

2 cups coarsely crushed pretzel sticks

Parchment paper

CRANBERRY-PISTACHIO COOKIES

1 cup butter, softened

¾ cup granulated sugar

¾ cup firmly packed light brown sugar

½ tsp. almond extract

2 large eggs

2¼ cups all-purpose flour

1 tsp. baking powder

1 tsp. table salt

2 cups chopped fresh cranberries

1 cup toasted coarsely chopped shelled raw pistachios

Cookie Frosting (page 104)

HANDS-ON 8 MIN. TOTAL 30 MIN.

Combine tart red cranberries and toasted green pistachios for a fresh twist and a festive holiday color combo. You'll love the texture and flavors of these cookies.

1. Preheat oven to 375°F. Beat butter at medium speed with an electric mixer until creamy; gradually add sugars, beating until blended. Add almond extract and eggs, beating until blended.

2. Combine flour, baking powder, and salt in a medium bowl; gradually add flour mixture to butter mixture, beating at low speed until blended after each addition. Stir in cranberries and pistachios.

3. Drop dough by rounded tablespoonfuls onto ungreased baking sheets.

4. Bake, in batches, at 375°F for 9 to 11 minutes. Transfer to wire racks, and cool completely (about 20 minutes).

5. Spread cookies with frosting, and sprinkle with additional chopped pistachios and dried cranberries.

NOTE: Freeze unfrosted baked cookies up to 6 months.

MAKES 3½ dozen

⭐ PARTY PERFECT

These drop cookies are ideal for holiday giving. Be sure they are completely cool before stacking and sliding into a cellophane sleeve. Tie them off with a pretty red or green satin ribbon, and add a gift tag that has the recipe on the back.

FILLED COOKIES

THE SCOOP ON PERFECT FILLED COOKIES

Tips to add a surprise in every little bite any way you fill them.

1. Make a dent with your thumb, leaving a ½-inch rim to contain the desired filled center.

2. Spread filling with a knife or spatula for even filling in sandwich cookies.

3. Use a pastry bag fitted with a tip to pipe frosting for airy and decorative filling.

4. Spread filling on chilled wedges of rugelach dough, leaving a border; add toppings, and roll up from wide end to point.

CORNMEAL THUMBPRINTS

Hands-on 45 min. Total 4 hours, 25 min.

This cookie melds Southern cornbread with the tang of Tomato Jam.

1. Beat butter and powdered sugar at medium speed with a heavy-duty electric stand mixer until fluffy. Add egg yolk and vanilla; beat until blended.

2. Combine flour and next 4 ingredients in a small bowl; slowly add flour to butter mixture, beating at low speed until just blended. Turn dough out onto a floured surface; knead 4 times. Shape into a 1-inch-thick disk. Wrap in plastic; chill 2 to 24 hours.

3. Preheat oven to 350°F. Combine pecans and granulated sugar in a small bowl. Shape dough into 1-inch balls. Lightly beat egg white. Dip each ball into egg white; dredge in pecan mixture. Place 1 inch apart on parchment paper-lined baking sheets. Press thumb into each ball, forming an indentation.

4. Bake for 10 minutes. Remove from oven. Press indentations in again. Spoon ½ tsp. Tomato Jam into each indentation. Bake 10 more minutes or until golden brown. Cool on baking sheets 5 minutes. Transfer to a wire rack, and cool completely (about 20 minutes).

MAKES about 2 dozen

INGREDIENTS

½ cup butter, softened

½ cup powdered sugar

1 large egg, separated

1 tsp. vanilla extract

¾ cup all-purpose flour

¾ cup plain yellow cornmeal

1 tsp. loosely packed lemon zest

½ tsp. kosher salt

¼ tsp. ground nutmeg

½ cup lightly toasted chopped pecans

3 Tbsp. granulated sugar

Parchment paper

½ cup Tomato Jam

TOMATO JAM

Boil **1½ lb. tomatoes** in water for 1 minute to loosen skins. Drain. Shock in ice water; peel over a saucepan to collect juices. Core and chop tomatoes; place in saucepan. Stir in **1 cup sugar, ¼ cup apple cider vinegar, 1 Tbsp. orange zest, 3 Tbsp. orange juice, 1 Tbsp. grated ginger, 2 tsp. sea salt, 1 tsp. ground coriander,** and **4 whole cloves;** bring to a low boil over medium heat. Reduce heat to low; simmer 30 minutes or until thickened. Remove from heat and discard cloves. Mash with a potato masher. Let cool 20 minutes. Chill up to 1 month.

LEMON THUMBPRINT COOKIES

INGREDIENTS

1 cup butter, softened

1 cup powdered sugar

1 cup granulated sugar

2 large eggs

1 cup vegetable oil

¼ cup fresh lemon juice

5¼ cups all-purpose flour

1 tsp. cream of tartar

1 tsp. baking soda

¼ tsp. table salt

1 tsp. loosely packed lemon zest

Vegetable cooking spray

¾ cup plus 2 Tbsp. raspberry jam

Garnish: fresh raspberries

HANDS-ON 35 MIN. TOTAL 1 HOUR, 30 MIN.

Tart lemon and sweet raspberry jam collide in these classic thumbprint cookies with lots of bright briar-patch flavor.

1. Preheat oven to 350°F. Beat butter at medium speed with an electric mixer until fluffy; add sugars, beating until blended. Add eggs, oil, and lemon juice, beating until blended.

2. Combine flour and next 4 ingredients in a large bowl; gradually add flour mixture to butter mixture, beating until blended.

3. Shape dough into 1-inch balls; place about 2 inches apart on lightly greased (with cooking spray) baking sheets. Press thumb into each ball, forming an indentation.

4. Bake, in batches, at 350°F for 9 to 11 minutes or until set. (Do not brown.) Transfer to wire racks, and cool completely (about 30 minutes). Spoon ½ tsp. raspberry jam into each indentation.

MAKES about 7 dozen

BLACKBERRY THUMBPRINTS

Hands-on 45 min. Total 2 hours, 5 min.

Vines heavy with blackberries (and chiggers) are plentiful in the South, with bumper harvests ending up in blackberry preserves, washtub cobblers, and every pie, pudding, and muffin around. Little dollops of sweet preserves are the perfect filling for thumbprint cookies.

1. Preheat oven to 325°F. Process almonds in a food processor 30 seconds or until very finely ground.

2. Beat butter at medium speed with a heavy-duty electric stand mixer until creamy. Gradually add powdered sugar, beating until blended.

3. Combine flour, next 3 ingredients, and almonds in a medium bowl; gradually add flour mixture to butter mixture, beating until blended.

4. Shape dough into ¾-inch balls; place 2 inches apart on parchment paper-lined baking sheets. Press thumb into each ball, forming an indentation.

5. Bake, in batches, at 325°F for 12 to 15 minutes or until lightly browned around edges. Cool on baking sheets 2 minutes. Transfer to wire racks, and cool 30 minutes.

6. Spoon preserves into a zip-top plastic freezer bag. Snip 1 corner of bag to make a small hole. Pipe preserves into indentations.

MAKES about 5 dozen

INGREDIENTS

½ cup toasted slivered almonds

1 cup butter, softened

1 cup powdered sugar

2 cups all-purpose flour

¼ tsp. table salt

¼ tsp. ground cloves

¼ tsp. ground cinnamon

Parchment paper

½ cup seedless blackberry preserves

APPLE BUTTER-WALNUT THUMBPRINTS

HANDS-ON 40 MIN. TOTAL 1 HOUR, 40 MIN.

Easy Apple Butter adds great flavor, but store-bought apple butter boiled for 5 minutes to thicken may be substituted.

1. Preheat oven to 350°F. Beat powdered sugar and butter at high speed with a heavy-duty electric stand mixer 4 minutes or until fluffy. Add egg and vanilla, beating until blended.

2. Pulse flour and next 4 ingredients in a food processor 10 times or until nuts are ground; add flour mixture to butter mixture, beating at medium speed 30 seconds.

3. Drop dough by level tablespoonfuls 1 to 2 inches apart onto 3 parchment paper-lined baking sheets. Dip thumb in cold water, and press into each cookie, forming an indentation; fill each with ½ tsp. Easy Apple Butter.

4. Bake, in batches, at 350°F for 14 to 18 minutes or until lightly brown around edges. Transfer to wire racks, and cool completely (about 10 minutes). Drizzle caramel topping over cooled cookies.

MAKES about 3½ dozen

INGREDIENTS

1¼ cups powdered sugar

1 cup unsalted butter, softened

1 large egg

2 tsp. vanilla extract

2½ cups all-purpose flour

1 cup toasted walnuts

1 tsp. kosher salt

½ tsp. baking powder

½ tsp. ground cinnamon

Parchment paper

½ cup Easy Apple Butter

Caramel topping

EASY APPLE BUTTER

Cut **3 lb. sweet apples** into 1-inch pieces. Bring apples, **1 cup apple cider,** and **½ cup sugar** to a boil in a Dutch oven over high heat. Cover partially; boil 20 minutes or until tender and most of the liquid has evaporated, stirring every 5 minutes. Process apples and cooking liquid in a blender until smooth. Return to Dutch oven. Stir in **¾ tsp. ground cinnamon, ¼ tsp. ground cloves,** and an additional **1 cup sugar.** Boil over high heat. Reduce heat to low, and simmer, uncovered, stirring often, 15 minutes or until thickened. Cool 45 minutes before filling cookies. Refrigerate in airtight containers up to 2 months, or freeze up to 6 months.

CHICORY BLOSSOMS

Hands-on 30 min. Total 1 hour, 50 min.

These filled chicory-flavored drop cookies have small amounts of granulated and brown sugars because the coffee liqueur and dark chocolate kisses add sweetness.

1. Preheat oven to 375°F. Beat butter at medium speed with an electric mixer until creamy; gradually add sugars, beating until blended. Add coffee liqueur; beat until blended.

2. Combine flour and next 4 ingredients in a medium bowl; gradually add flour mixture to butter mixture, beating at low speed until blended. Stir in almonds. (If desired, refrigerate in an airtight container up to 1 week.)

3. Drop dough by heaping tablespoonfuls 2 inches apart onto parchment paper-lined baking sheets.

4. Bake, in batches, at 375°F for 10 to 12 minutes or until golden brown around edges. (Bake chilled dough 11 to 12 minutes.) Remove from oven, and immediately press 1 dark chocolate kiss into center of each cookie. Cool on baking sheets on a wire rack 3 minutes. Transfer to wire racks, and cool completely (about 1 hour).

*Toasted, slivered almonds or dry-roasted salted peanuts may be substituted for salted, roasted almonds.

NOTE: We tested with Community Coffee Instant Coffee and Chicory.

MAKES about 3½ dozen

SMART COOKIE

Southerners brewed ground roasted chicory root as a coffee replacement during wartime scarcity. In Louisiana, chicory and coffee-chicory blends remain prevalent today.

INGREDIENTS

1 cup butter, softened

6 Tbsp. granulated sugar

¼ cup firmly packed light brown sugar

½ cup coffee liqueur

2⅔ cups all-purpose flour

2 tsp. instant coffee and chicory

1 tsp. baking soda

½ tsp. ground cinnamon

¼ tsp. table salt

1 cup chopped salted, roasted almonds*

Parchment paper

42 dark chocolate kisses

LEMON MERINGUE SANDWICH COOKIES

INGREDIENTS

Cookies:

1 cup butter, softened

¾ cup granulated sugar

½ cup powdered sugar

2 large eggs

1 tsp. vanilla extract

1⅓ cups all-purpose flour

1¼ cups pastry flour

1 cup graham cracker crumbs (about 11 crackers)

1 tsp. table salt

Parchment paper

1 large egg white, lightly beaten

Coarse sanding sugar

Meringue Filling (page 95)

1 cup lemon curd

Hands-on 40 min. Total 5 hours, 30 min.

A stiff lemon curd works best for this recipe. Use pretty fluted or scalloped cutters to add interest to the edges of this brightly-flavored treat.

1. Prepare Cookies: Beat butter at medium speed with an electric mixer until creamy; gradually add sugars, beating until fluffy. Add eggs, 1 at a time, beating until blended. Beat in vanilla.

2. Combine flours, graham cracker crumbs, and salt in a large bowl; gradually add flour mixture to butter mixture, beating at low speed just until blended after each addition. Divide dough in half; flatten each portion into a disk. Wrap in plastic, and refrigerate 2 hours or until firm.

3. Preheat oven to 350°F. Roll each portion of dough to ⅛-inch thickness on a lightly floured surface. Cut dough with a 2½-inch fluted round cutter; place 1 inch apart on parchment paper-lined baking sheets. Press a 2-inch fluted round cutter into centers, being careful not to cut all the way through dough. Brush rim of dough circle with egg white, and sprinkle with sanding sugar.

4. Bake at 350°F for 12 to 15 minutes or until golden brown around edges. Cool on baking sheets 5 minutes. Transfer to wire racks, and cool completely (about 30 minutes).

5. Spoon Meringue Filling into a large piping bag fitted with a large star tip; pipe in a swirl pattern on bottom half of cookies (20 cookies). Spoon curd over filling. Top with remaining cookies to create a sandwich. Let stand 2 hours or until filling is set.

MAKES 20 cookies

LINZER COOKIES

Hands-on 30 min. Total 2 hours, 30 min.

Linzer Cookies are great for the holidays and look just as good as they taste. A dough scraper, which can be purchased inexpensively at kitchen stores, makes transferring these festive cutouts onto baking sheets a breeze.

1. Beat butter at medium speed with an electric mixer; gradually add 1 cup powdered sugar, beating until light and fluffy.

2. Combine flour and next 5 ingredients in a medium bowl; gradually add flour mixture to butter mixture, beating just until blended.

3. Divide dough into 2 equal portions. Wrap in plastic, and chill 1 hour.

4. Preheat oven to 325°F. Roll each dough portion to a ⅛-inch thickness on a lightly floured surface; cut with a 3-inch round- or square-shaped cutter. Cut centers out of half of cookies with a 1½-inch round- or square-shaped cutter. Place all circles or squares on lightly greased (with cooking spray) baking sheets.

5. Bake, in batches, at 325°F for 15 minutes. Transfer to wire racks, and cool completely (about 30 minutes). Spread jam onto each solid cookie. Sprinkle remaining circles or squares with powdered sugar; top each solid cookie with a hollow circle or square.

MAKES 3 dozen

INGREDIENTS

1¼ cups butter, softened

1 cup powdered sugar, sifted

2½ cups all-purpose flour

½ cup toasted finely chopped pecans

¼ tsp. table salt

¼ tsp. ground cloves

¼ tsp. ground cinnamon

1 tsp. loosely packed lemon zest

Vegetable cooking spray

¼ cup seedless raspberry jam

Additional powdered sugar

PECAN LINZER COOKIES

Use your favorite jams to vary the flavor and color of these delicious beauties. We used peach and raspberry.

INGREDIENTS

1 cup butter, very soft

⅓ cup granulated sugar

1 tsp. loosely packed lemon zest

1 large egg

1 large egg yolk

2¼ cups all-purpose flour

1 cup pecan halves

1 tsp. ground cinnamon

½ tsp. ground cloves

Parchment paper

¾ cup fruit jam

1. Beat butter, sugar, and zest at medium speed with an electric mixer 1 minute. Add egg and egg yolk; beat 30 seconds until blended. Scrape bowl; beat 30 seconds.

2. Pulse flour and next 3 ingredients in a food processor until finely ground; gradually add flour mixture to butter mixture, beating until blended.

3. Shape dough into 2 (½-inch-thick) rectangles. Wrap each rectangle in plastic, and chill 4 hours to 3 days.

4. Preheat oven to 350°F. Generously flour both sides of dough; place on parchment paper. Roll each into a 14- x 10-inch rectangle. Cut each rectangle into 24 squares with a lightly floured 2-inch scalloped square cutter, rerolling scraps as needed. Chill on parchment paper 30 minutes.

5. Place cookies 1 inch apart on parchment paper-lined baking sheets. Cut centers out of half of cookies with a lightly floured 1¼-inch square- or flower-shaped cutter. (If desired, place dough centers on a parchment paper-lined baking sheet; chill 15 minutes, and bake as directed.)

6. Bake, in batches, at 350°F for 12 to 14 minutes or until golden brown around edges. Cool on parchment paper on a wire rack.

7. Spread ¼ tsp. jam onto each solid cookie; top with hollow cookies.

MAKES about 2 dozen

PEACH-PECAN RUGELACH

HANDS-ON 1 HOUR, 15 MIN. TOTAL 3 HOURS

Rugelach, a traditional Hanukkah treat, are small crescent-shaped cookies made with cream cheese dough surrounding various fillings. Southern favorites—peach preserves and chopped pecans—fill these tasty treats.

1. Preheat oven to 375°F. Pulse flour and next 3 ingredients in a food processor 3 or 4 times until dough forms a small ball and pulls away from sides of bowl. Divide dough into 8 equal portions, shaping each portion into a ball. Wrap each ball separately in plastic, and chill 1 to 24 hours.

2. Place preserves in a small saucepan over medium heat. Cook, stirring often, 2 to 3 minutes or until warm.

3. Roll 1 dough ball at a time into an 8-inch circle on a lightly floured surface. Brush dough with 1 to 2 Tbsp. warm preserves; sprinkle with 2 Tbsp. pecans. Cut circle into 8 wedges; roll up wedges, starting at wide end, to form a crescent shape. Place, point side down, on a lightly greased (with cooking spray) parchment paper-lined baking sheet. Repeat procedure with remaining dough balls, preserves, and pecans.

4. Combine sugar and cinnamon; sprinkle over crescents.

5. Bake at 375°F for 15 to 20 minutes or until golden brown. Transfer to wire racks, and cool completely (about 20 minutes).

MAKES 5 dozen

INGREDIENTS

2¼ cups all-purpose flour

1 cup butter, cut into pieces

1 (8-oz.) package cream cheese, cut into pieces

½ tsp. table salt

1 (12-oz.) jar peach preserves

1 cup toasted chopped pecans

Vegetable cooking spray

Parchment paper

3 Tbsp. sugar

2 tsp. ground cinnamon

SWEETHEART JAMWICHES

INGREDIENTS

1 (14.1-oz.) package refrigerated piecrusts

1 large egg white, lightly beaten

¼ cup coarse sanding sugar

Parchment paper

1 (3-oz.) package cream cheese, softened

¼ cup powdered sugar

3 Tbsp. butter, softened, divided

½ tsp. almond extract

½ (10-oz.) jar seedless raspberry preserves or strawberry jam

½ cup white chocolate morsels

HANDS-ON 30 MIN. TOTAL 1 HOUR, 30 MIN.

Store-bought piecrust is the ideal base for these sweet cookies. The almond extract-kissed cream cheese filling is topped with seedless raspberry jam and takes this giftable cookie from delicious to swoon-worthy.

1. Preheat oven to 400°F. Unroll piecrusts on a lightly floured surface. Cut each piecrust with a 2-inch heart-shaped cookie cutter, rerolling scraps as needed to equal 46 pastry hearts. Brush 1 side of each heart with egg white, and sprinkle with sanding sugar. Place hearts on 2 ungreased baking sheets.

2. Bake, in batches, at 400°F for 7 to 8 minutes or until lightly browned. Transfer to wire racks placed over parchment paper, and cool completely (about 30 minutes).

3. Beat cream cheese, powdered sugar, 2 Tbsp. butter, and almond extract at medium speed with an electric mixer until blended.

4. Spread cream cheese mixture evenly on unsugared sides of half the hearts; spread about ½ tsp. preserves over mixture. Top with remaining hearts, unsugared sides down.

5. Microwave white chocolate morsels and remaining 1 Tbsp. butter in a small microwave-safe bowl at HIGH 1 minute or until melted and smooth, stirring after 30 seconds. Spoon mixture into a small zip-top plastic freezer bag; seal bag. Snip 1 corner of bag to make a tiny hole. Drizzle a small amount of chocolate over each heart. Let stand 30 minutes or until set.

MAKES about 2 dozen

PARTY PERFECT

Serve these heart-shaped sweets for Valentine's Day in a pretty box lined with pink tissue paper and tied with a red satin bow.

STRAWBERRY SHORTCAKE SANDWICH COOKIES

Hands-on 30 min. Total 2 hours, 20 min.

These portable cookies are perfect for a picnic or cookout.

1. Prepare Cookies: Preheat oven to 375°F. Beat butter at medium speed with an electric mixer until creamy; gradually add granulated sugar, beating until fluffy. Add egg, beating until blended. Beat in vanilla and lemon zest.

2. Combine flour, baking soda, and salt in a medium bowl; gradually add flour mixture to butter mixture alternately with sour cream, beating at low speed just until blended after each addition.

3. Drop dough by rounded tablespoonfuls 2 inches apart onto parchment paper-lined baking sheets. Sprinkle generously with sanding sugar.

4. Bake at 375°F for 11 to 13 minutes or until puffed and lightly browned around edges. Cool on baking sheets 5 minutes. Transfer to wire racks, and cool completely (about 30 minutes).

5. Prepare Meringue Filling: Bring first 3 ingredients and 3 Tbsp. water to a boil in a small, heavy saucepan over medium-high heat, stirring just until sugar dissolves. Cook, without stirring, until a candy thermometer registers 240°F (about 4 minutes). Beat egg whites and cream of tartar at high speed with an electric mixer until soft peaks form. Gradually pour hot sugar syrup into egg white mixture, beating first at medium speed and then at high speed; beat in vanilla. Continue beating for 5 minutes or until mixture is thick, glossy, and the texture of marshmallow fluff.

6. Spoon filling into a piping bag fitted with a medium star tip; pipe onto bottoms of cookies. Spoon 1 Tbsp. jam onto filling on half of frosted cookies. Top with remaining frosted cookies to create a sandwich. Let stand 1 hour or until filling is set.

MAKES about 1¼ dozen

INGREDIENTS

Cookies:
½ cup butter, softened
1 cup granulated sugar
1 large egg
1 tsp. vanilla extract
1 tsp. loosely packed lemon zest
2 cups all-purpose flour
½ tsp. baking soda
¼ tsp. table salt
½ cup sour cream
Parchment paper
Coarse sanding sugar
Meringue Filling:
½ cup granulated sugar
⅓ cup light corn syrup
⅛ tsp. table salt
2 large egg whites
¼ tsp. cream of tartar
½ tsp. vanilla extract
Remaining ingredient:
1 cup seedless strawberry jam

PEANUT BUTTER-TOFFEE TURTLE COOKIES

Hands-on 15 min. Total 1 hour, 30 min.

These start as drop cookies and finish as turtle candies with every indulgent flavor imaginable.

1. Preheat oven to 350°F. Beat first 4 ingredients at medium speed with an electric mixer until creamy. Add egg, beating until blended. Add baking mix, beating at low speed just until blended. Stir in toffee bits, chopped peanuts, and ⅔ cup chocolate morsels.

2. Drop dough by rounded tablespoonfuls onto ungreased baking sheets; flatten dough with hand.

3. Bake, in batches, at 350°F for 10 to 12 minutes or until golden brown. Cool cookies on baking sheets 1 minute. Transfer to wire racks, and cool completely (about 20 minutes).

4. Microwave caramels and 2 Tbsp. cream in a microwave-safe bowl at HIGH 1 minute; stir. Continue to microwave at 30-second intervals, stirring until caramels melt and mixture is smooth, adding remaining cream, if necessary. Stir in vanilla. Spoon caramel mixture evenly onto tops of cookies.

5. Microwave remaining ⅔ cup chocolate morsels in a small microwave-safe bowl at HIGH 1 minute or until melted and smooth, stirring after 30 seconds. Drizzle chocolate evenly over cookies. Let stand 30 minutes or until set.

MAKES 3 dozen

SMART COOKIE

Pour melted chocolate into a zip-top plastic freezer bag. Snip a tiny hole in the bottom corner, and gently twist the bag to pipe the melted chocolate onto the cookies. The chocolate drizzle will harden as it cools.

INGREDIENTS

½ cup unsalted butter, softened

½ cup granulated sugar

½ cup firmly packed light brown sugar

⅔ cup creamy peanut butter

1 large egg

2 cups all-purpose baking mix

⅔ cup almond toffee bits

⅔ cup coarsely chopped peanuts

1⅓ cup milk chocolate morsels, divided

1 (11-oz.) package vanilla caramels

2 to 3 Tbsp. whipping cream

½ tsp. vanilla extract

DATE MOONS

HANDS-ON 20 MIN. TOTAL 2 HOURS, 20 MIN.

Chewy dates are the sweet surprise enveloped in these little crescent-shaped cookies. If you love a fig bar, you'll flip for this filled cookie.

1. Beat butter and cream cheese at medium speed with an electric mixer until creamy. Add flour and salt, and beat until blended.

2. Shape dough into a ball. Wrap in plastic, and chill 1 hour.

3. Cook dates, granulated sugar, and ¼ cup water in a saucepan over medium heat 3 to 5 minutes or until thickened. Remove from heat; stir in walnuts and orange zest, and let cool.

4. Preheat oven to 375°F. Divide dough in half. Roll 1 portion to ⅛-inch thickness on a lightly floured surface. Cut dough with a 2½-inch round-shaped cutter, and place on a lightly greased (with cooking spray) baking sheet. Spoon ½ tsp. date mixture in center of each circle. Repeat procedure with remaining dough and date mixture.

5. Fold dough over filling, pressing edges with tines of a fork to seal.

6. Bake, in batches, at 375°F for 15 minutes or until lightly browned. Transfer to wire racks, and cool completely (about 30 minutes). Sprinkle with powdered sugar.

MAKES 3 dozen

INGREDIENTS

½ cup butter, softened

1 (3-oz.) package cream cheese, softened

1 cup all-purpose flour

⅛ tsp. table salt

1 cup chopped dates

¼ cup granulated sugar

½ cup chopped walnuts

1 tsp. orange zest

Vegetable cooking spray

½ cup powdered sugar

PECAN PIE COOKIES

These pecan pie cookies pack the sweet nutty flavors of traditional pecan pie into bite-size indulgences perfect for holiday gatherings.

INGREDIENTS

1¼ cups butter, softened, divided

½ cup granulated sugar

½ cup plus 3 Tbsp. dark corn syrup, divided

2 large eggs, separated

2½ cups all-purpose flour

½ cup powdered sugar

¾ cup finely chopped pecans

Vegetable cooking spray

1. Beat 1 cup butter and sugar at medium speed with an electric mixer until light and fluffy. Add ½ cup corn syrup and egg yolks, beating until blended. Gradually stir in flour; cover and chill 1 hour.

2. Melt ¼ cup butter in a heavy saucepan over medium heat; stir in powdered sugar and 3 Tbsp. corn syrup. Cook, stirring often, until mixture boils. Remove from heat. Stir in pecans; chill 30 minutes. Shape into ¼-inch balls (about ¼ tsp. mixture per ball); set aside.

3. Preheat oven to 375°F. Shape dough into 1-inch balls; place 2 inches apart on lightly greased (with cooking spray) baking sheets. Beat egg whites until foamy; brush on dough balls.

4. Bake, in batches, at 375°F for 6 minutes. Remove from oven, and place pecan balls in center of each cookie. Bake 8 to 10 more minutes or until lightly browned. Cool on baking sheets 5 minutes. Transfer to wire racks, and cool completely (about 30 minutes). Freeze up to 1 month, if desired.

MAKES 4½ dozen

COOKIE PRESS SANDWICHES

Hands-on 2 hours Total 2 hours, 45 min.

Pick your favorite filling flavor for this classic sandwich cookie. We tested with peppermint, orange, and lemon extracts. To make them even more festive, tint the filling with liquid food coloring.

1. Preheat oven to 400°F. Beat 1 cup butter and next 3 ingredients at medium speed with an electric mixer 1 minute. Add egg, and beat 30 seconds.

2. Sift together flour and salt. Add flour mixture to butter mixture, and beat at low speed 30 seconds. Scrape sides of bowl, and beat 15 more seconds. Divide dough into 3 equal portions.

3. Following manufacturer's instructions, use a cookie press fitted with desired disk to shape dough into cookies, spacing cookies 1½ inches apart on 2 ungreased baking sheets.

4. Bake at 400°F for 7 minutes, placing 1 baking sheet on middle oven rack and 1 sheet on lower oven rack. Rotate baking sheets front to back and top rack to bottom rack. Bake 1 to 2 more minutes or until golden brown around edges. Transfer cookies to a wire rack, and cool completely (about 10 minutes). Repeat with remaining dough.

5. Beat remaining ½ cup butter, powdered sugar and 3 Tbsp. milk at medium speed 2 minutes. Add flavored extract; beat at low speed until well blended. Add remaining 1 Tbsp. milk, if necessary.

6. Spoon filling into a zip-top plastic freezer bag. (Do not seal.) Snip 1 corner of bag to make a small hole. Pipe filling onto bottoms of half of cookies. Top with remaining cookies to create a sandwich. Sprinkle with powdered sugar. Serve immediately, or let stand 2 hours. Store in an airtight container up to 2 weeks.

MAKES 3 dozen

INGREDIENTS

1½ cups butter, softened, divided

½ cup granulated sugar

½ tsp. almond extract

½ tsp. vanilla extract

1 large egg

2¼ cups all-purpose flour

½ tsp. table salt

1 (16-oz.) package powdered sugar

3 to 4 Tbsp. milk

¾ tsp. flavored extract (such as peppermint, lemon, or orange)

½ cup powdered sugar

ITALIAN CHRISTMAS COOKIES

INGREDIENTS

4½ cups all-purpose flour

2 tsp. baking powder

1¼ cups shortening

¾ cup sugar

⅓ cup milk

1 tsp. vanilla extract

3 large eggs, well beaten

3 (8-oz.) packages dried figs

Shortening

Cookie Frosting

Coarse sanding sugar

HANDS-ON 15 MIN. TOTAL 1 HOUR, 30 MIN.

These traditional Italian Christmas Cookies are filled with dried figs, topped with a sweet white icing, and covered in sprinkles or sanding sugars. Serve these any time of year.

1. Preheat oven to 350°F. Combine flour and baking powder in a large bowl. Cut shortening into flour mixture with a pastry blender or fork until mixture resembles coarse meal. Make a well in center of mixture; set aside.

2. Combine sugar and milk in a small saucepan over medium heat. Cook, stirring constantly, until sugar dissolves. Remove from heat; stir in vanilla. Gradually stir in eggs. Add to dry flour mixture, stirring just until moistened.

3. Turn dough out onto a lightly floured surface, and knead 3 to 4 times. Roll to ¼-inch thickness; cut into 1½-inch squares. Place a fig in the center of each square; press dough around fig. Place cookies, seam side down, on greased (with shortening) baking sheets.

4. Bake, in batches, at 350°F for 12 to 15 minutes. Transfer to wire racks, and cool completely (about 30 minutes). Spread Cookie Frosting over tops of cookies, and sprinkle with sanding sugar.

MAKES about 10 dozen

COOKIE FROSTING

Beat **2 Tbsp. softened butter** at medium speed with an electric mixer until creamy; gradually add **2 cups sifted powdered sugar,** beating until blended. Add **2 Tbsp. milk,** and beat until smooth. Tint with **food coloring** as desired.

FRUIT-FILLED COOKIES

HANDS-ON 30 MIN. TOTAL 1 HOUR, 30 MIN.

We loved this unique yeast cookie dough so much that we made a variation called Snowflake Cookies (below).

1. Combine first 3 ingredients in a large bowl. Cut butter into flour mixture with a pastry blender or 2 forks until crumbly.

2. Combine yeast and warm milk in a 1-cup glass measuring cup; let stand 10 minutes. Stir in egg and vanilla. Add yeast mixture to flour mixture, stirring until dry ingredients are moistened. Divide dough into 4 equal portions. Wrap each portion in plastic, and chill 30 minutes.

3. Preheat oven to 350°F. Roll 1 portion of dough to ⅛-inch thickness on a flat surface lightly dusted with powdered sugar. Cut into 3-inch squares. Spoon 1 heaping tsp. peach or cherry dessert filling in center of square. Fold 2 opposite corners to center, slightly overlapping. Place on parchment paper-lined baking sheets. Repeat procedure with remaining dough and filling.

4. Bake, in batches, at 350°F for 18 to 20 minutes or until lightly browned. Cool on baking sheets 5 minutes. Transfer to wire racks, and cool completely (about 30 minutes). Sprinkle cookies with powdered sugar.

MAKES 3 dozen

COOKIE SWAP

Snowflake Cookies: Omit dessert filling. Prepare and roll out dough as directed. Cut dough with a 3¾-inch snowflake-shaped cookie cutter. Place on parchment paper-lined baking sheets. Sprinkle with sparkling sugar. Bake at 350°F for 10 minutes or until lightly browned. Cool cookies as directed. Makes about 5 dozen.

INGREDIENTS

3 cups all-purpose flour

1 Tbsp. granulated sugar

½ tsp. table salt

1 cup butter, cut into pieces

1 (¼-oz.) envelope active dry yeast

½ cup warm milk (100°F to 110°F)

1 large egg, lightly beaten

½ tsp. vanilla extract

Powdered sugar

1 (12-oz.) can peach or cherry dessert filling

Parchment paper

BLACKBERRY SWIRL MERINGUE COOKIES

3 large egg whites

¼ tsp. cream of tartar

⅛ tsp. table salt

⅔ cup sugar

¼ tsp. vanilla extract

Parchment paper

⅓ cup seedless blackberry jam

Hands-on 15 min. Total 3 hours, 15 min.

Many Southerners refer to blackberries as "dewberries" and enjoy summer's bumper crops in cobblers and pies. Made with jam, these light and airy cookies may be enjoyed throughout the year.

1. Preheat oven to 200°F. Beat first 3 ingredients at high speed with an electric mixer until foamy. Gradually add sugar, 1 Tbsp. at a time, beating until stiff, glossy peaks form and sugar dissolves (about 6 minutes). Beat in vanilla.

2. Spoon mixture into 18 mounds on 2 parchment paper-lined baking sheets. Spread each mound gently to about 2½ inches in diameter. Stir jam to loosen (pourable consistency). Top each meringue with about ¾ tsp. jam; use an offset spatula or knife to gently swirl jam into meringues.

3. Bake at 200°F for 2½ hours or until meringues are dry and crisp around the edges but still slightly soft in the center, and can be removed from paper without sticking to fingers. Transfer to wire racks, and cool completely (about 30 minutes).

MAKES 1½ dozen

SMART COOKIE

If you prefer your meringues to be crisp and dry from center to exterior, turn the oven off after baking and let them stand in the oven overnight.

CREAM-FILLED CHOCOLATE CHIP WAFERS

Hands-on 20 min. Total 2 hours, 20 min.

It's great to have an easy, no-bake cookie recipe in your repertoire. Simply sandwich this chunky, homemade filling between purchased chocolate wafers, and chill. You will win hearts in no time.

1. Beat first 3 ingredients at medium speed with an electric mixer until creamy. Gradually add sugars, beating until blended. Stir in chocolate morsels and pecans.

2. Spread about 1 Tbsp. cream cheese mixture evenly onto 1 side of half of wafers. Top with remaining wafers to create a sandwich. Cover cookies, and chill 2 hours. Store in refrigerator.

NOTE: We tested with Nabisco Famous Chocolate Wafers.

MAKES about 3½ dozen

COOKIE SWAP

Go wild with variations on this cookie recipe by sandwiching this rich-and-creamy filling between your favorite store-brought cookie—oatmeal, chocolate chip, shortbread, or vanilla wafers.

INGREDIENTS

1 (8-oz.) package ⅓-less-fat cream cheese, softened

⅓ cup butter, softened

¼ tsp. vanilla extract

¾ cup powdered sugar

2 Tbsp. brown sugar

¾ cup semisweet chocolate mini-morsels

¾ cup toasted finely chopped pecans

2 (9-oz.) boxes chocolate wafers

CARAMEL-FILLED CHOCOLATE COOKIES

Hands-on 15 min. Total 1 hour, 30 min.

This may be gilding the cookie, but it's worth every step of the process. Pecan-studded dough encases pieces of chocolate-caramel cookie bars and gets sprinkled with more pecans for good measure before baking. Try to eat just one.

INGREDIENTS

1 cup butter, softened

1 cup plus 1 Tbsp. granulated sugar, divided

1 cup firmly packed brown sugar

2 large eggs

2 tsp. vanilla extract

2¼ cups all-purpose flour

¾ cup unsweetened cocoa

1 tsp. baking soda

1 cup chopped pecans, divided

6 (2-oz.) packages chocolate-caramel cookie bars, cut into 1-inch pieces

Parchment paper

1. Preheat oven to 375°F. Beat butter at medium speed with an electric mixer until creamy; gradually add 1 cup granulated sugar and brown sugar, beating until blended. Add eggs, 1 at a time, beating until blended after each addition. Beat in vanilla.

2. Combine flour, cocoa, and baking soda in a medium bowl; gradually add flour mixture to butter mixture, beating at low speed until blended after each addition. Stir in ½ cup pecans. Shape 1 Tbsp. dough around each candy piece, covering completely, to form balls.

3. Combine remaining ½ cup pecans and remaining 1 Tbsp. sugar. Gently press the top of each ball into pecan mixture. Place balls, pecan sides up, 2 inches apart on parchment paper-lined baking sheets.

4. Bake, in batches, at 375°F for 7 to 10 minutes. Cool on baking sheets 2 minutes. Transfer to wire racks, and cool completely (about 30 minutes).

NOTE: We tested with Twix Caramel Cookie Bars.

MAKES 4 dozen

MARBLE-CINNAMON SANDWICH COOKIES

Hands-on 45 min. Total 1 hour, 50 min.

Seek out a Southern-made peanut butter, like Reginald's Homemade or Naturally More. Use the bottom of a half-cup measuring cup to flatten the cookies to the perfect size.

1. Combine 2 cups flour, 1¼ tsp. cream of tartar, ¾ tsp. baking soda, and ¼ tsp. salt in a medium bowl. Combine cocoa and remaining 1⅔ cups flour, 1¼ tsp. cream of tartar, ¾ tsp. baking soda, and ¼ tsp. salt in a separate medium bowl.

2. Beat butter, vanilla, 2 cups sugar, and 1 tsp. cinnamon at medium speed with an electric mixer until creamy. Add eggs, 1 at a time, beating until blended after each addition. Spoon half of butter mixture into cocoa mixture, beat until blended. Spoon remaining butter mixture into flour mixture; beat until blended. Cover and chill 30 minutes.

3. Preheat oven to 350°F. Combine remaining ⅓ cup sugar and 3 tsp. cinnamon in a small bowl. Drop plain dough by level tablespoonfuls onto aluminum foil. Top each with 1 Tbsp. chocolate dough; roll together into a ball. Roll in cinnamon-sugar; place 3 inches apart on parchment paper-lined baking sheets, and flatten.

4. Bake, in batches, at 350°F for 14 minutes or until lightly browned around edges, lightly tapping baking sheets halfway through to deflate cookies. Cool on baking sheets 5 minutes. Transfer to wire racks, and cool completely (about 30 minutes).

5. Spread about 2 Tbsp. peanut butter onto one side of half of cookies. Top with remaining cookies to create a sandwich.

MAKES about 1¼ dozen

INGREDIENTS

3⅔ cups all-purpose flour, divided

2½ tsp. cream of tartar, divided

1½ tsp. baking soda, divided

½ tsp. kosher salt, divided

⅓ cup unsweetened cocoa

1¾ cups butter, softened

2½ tsp. vanilla extract

2⅓ cups sugar, divided

4 tsp. ground cinnamon, divided

3 large eggs

Parchment paper

2 cups cinnamon-raisin swirl peanut butter

INGREDIENTS

½ cup butter, softened

½ cup granulated sugar

½ cup firmly packed light brown sugar

1 large egg

1 tsp. vanilla extract

1 cup all-purpose flour

½ tsp. baking powder

½ tsp. baking soda

½ tsp. table salt

1 cup graham cracker crumbs

1 (8-oz.) container sour cream

Parchment paper

Marshmallow Filling

1 (12-oz.) package semisweet chocolate morsels

2 tsp. shortening

Toppings: chopped roasted salted almonds, chopped crystallized ginger, sea salt

SWOON PIES

HANDS-ON 45 MIN. TOTAL 2 HOURS, 40 MIN.

These are our take on the iconic marshmallow-filled pastry.

1. Preheat oven to 350°F. Beat butter and next 2 ingredients with an electric mixer until fluffy. Add egg and vanilla; beat until blended.

2. Sift together flour and next 3 ingredients in a medium bowl; stir in graham cracker crumbs. Add flour mixture to butter mixture alternately with sour cream. Beat at low speed just until blended after each addition, stopping to scrape bowl as needed. Drop batter by rounded tablespoonfuls 2 inches apart onto parchment paper-lined baking sheets.

3. Bake, in batches, at 350°F for 15 minutes or until set and bottoms are golden brown. Transfer (on parchment paper) to wire racks to cool completely (about 30 minutes).

4. Spread 1 heaping Tbsp. Marshmallow Filling onto flat sides of half of cookies. Top with remaining cookies, flat sides down, to create a sandwich. Freeze on a parchment paper-lined baking sheet 30 minutes or until filling is set. Remove cookies from freezer, and let stand 10 minutes.

5. Microwave chocolate morsels and shortening in a microwave-safe bowl at HIGH 1 minute or until melted, stirring halfway through. Dip half of each cookie sandwich into melted chocolate. Place on a parchment paper-lined baking sheet. Sprinkle with desired toppings, and freeze 10 minutes or until chocolate is set.

MAKES 1 dozen

MARSHMALLOW FILLING

Beat ½ cup softened butter at medium speed with an electric mixer until creamy; add 1 cup sifted powdered sugar, beating until blended. Add ½ cup marshmallow crème and ½ tsp. vanilla extract, and beat until blended.

PEANUT BUTTER-CARAMEL CANDY BITES

Hands-on 20 min. Total 35 min.

Use refrigerated dough as the base for these colorful candy-filled peanut butter cookies. Kids will love helping make these—right before they gobble them up.

1. Preheat oven to 350°F. Shape dough into 24 (1-inch) balls; place in a lightly greased 24-cup miniature muffin pan.

2. Bake at 350°F for 15 to 18 minutes or until lightly browned around edges. Remove from oven, and press 1 bite-size chocolate-covered caramel-peanut nougat bar into each cookie; cool completely in pan. Sprinkle cookies evenly with candy-coated chocolate pieces.

NOTE: We tested with Snickers and M&M's.

MAKES 2 dozen

⭐ PARTY PERFECT

These bite-size whimsical treats are perfectly portioned for kids' birthday parties. Pick candy in colors that fit your theme.

INGREDIENTS

1 (16.5-oz.) package refrigerated peanut butter cookie dough

24 bite-size chocolate-covered caramel-peanut nougat bars

72 candy-coated chocolate pieces

PEPPERMINT SANDWICH COOKIES

Make an easy peppermint filling with ready-to-spread vanilla frosting, peppermint candy, and peppermint extract to spread between purchased chocolate wafers. You can make these cookies ahead and keep them in the refrigerator for up to 8 hours (they will soften slightly).

Combine first 3 ingredients in a small bowl. Spread mixture evenly on one side of half of chocolate wafers. Top with remaining chocolate wafers to create a sandwich. Press crushed peppermint into the edges of the filling.

MAKES 10 cookies

INGREDIENTS

⅔ cup ready-to-spread vanilla frosting

3 Tbsp. crushed hard peppermint candy

¼ tsp. peppermint extract

20 chocolate wafers

1 cup finely crushed peppermint

SMART COOKIE

Extracts are a baker's secret weapon, and a little bit goes a long way when it comes to flavoring dough. The essence or oils are extracted from dried or fresh leaves, flowers, or seeds and blended with an alcohol base. Look for pure or natural extracts for authentic flavor you can feel good about.

ROLLED COOKIES

THE SCOOP ON PERFECT ROLLED COOKIES

Learn how to roll your way to great results.

1. Roll chilled dough evenly for cutting.

2. If edges get too thin or uneven, use a pastry scraper to straighten.

3. Use parchment paper to form slice-and-bake dough into a log for cutting.

4. Rolling dough with palms creates perfect rounds. Chill before baking to firm up.

TEA CAKES

Hands-on 30 min. Total 2 hours, 30 min.

Even though they're called cakes, tea cakes are old-fashioned cookies made with butter, sugar, eggs, flour, and vanilla. They're perfect with afternoon tea or a glass of ice-cold lemonade. For a decadent spin, spread Cream Cheese Frosting (page 208) and your favorite jam or preserves onto each cookie.

1. Beat butter at medium speed with an electric mixer until creamy; gradually add sugar, beating until blended. Add eggs, 1 at a time, beating until blended after each addition. Add vanilla, beating until blended.

2. Combine flour, baking soda, and salt in medium bowl; gradually add flour mixture to butter mixture, beating at low speed until blended after each addition.

3. Divide dough in half. Wrap each portion in plastic, and chill 1 hour.

4. Preheat oven to 350°F. Roll each portion of dough to ¼-inch thickness on a lightly floured surface. Cut dough with a 2½-inch round-shaped cutter; place 1 inch apart on parchment paper-lined baking sheets.

5. Bake, in batches, at 350°F for 10 to 12 minutes or until lightly browned around edges. Cool on baking sheet 5 minutes. Transfer to wire racks, and cool completely (about 30 minutes).

MAKES 3 dozen

INGREDIENTS

1 cup butter, softened

2 cups sugar

3 large eggs

1 tsp. vanilla extract

3½ cups all-purpose flour

1 tsp. baking soda

½ tsp. table salt

Parchment paper

LEMON-POPPY SEED COOKIES

HANDS-ON 20 MIN. TOTAL 9 HOURS, 40 MIN.

These treats are just like the marvelous morning muffin in cookie form. You can freeze the dough up to two months, and then thaw and bake when the craving strikes.

INGREDIENTS

1 cup butter, softened

1 cup granulated sugar

1 cup firmly packed light brown sugar

2 large eggs

1 tsp. loosely packed lemon zest

2 Tbsp. fresh lemon juice

3½ cups all-purpose flour

1 tsp. baking soda

2 tsp. poppy seeds

½ tsp. table salt

Wax paper

Vegetable cooking spray

1. Beat butter and sugars at medium speed with an electric mixer until fluffy. Add eggs, 1 at a time, beating until blended after each addition. Add lemon zest and lemon juice, beating until blended.

2. Combine flour, baking soda, poppy seeds, and salt in a medium bowl; gradually add flour mixture to butter mixture, beating just until blended.

3. Divide dough into 3 equal portions; place each portion on wax paper. Roll each into a 12-inch log. Cover and chill 8 hours.

4. Preheat oven to 350°F. Cut each log into 28 (½-inch-thick) slices, and place on lightly greased (with cooking spray) baking sheets.

5. Bake, in batches, at 350°F for 12 to 14 minutes or until lightly browned around edges. Transfer to wire racks, and cool completely (about 30 minutes).

MAKES 7 dozen

SMART COOKIE

While it's true that poppy seeds come from the same variety of poppy from which opium is harvested, the seeds have negligible traces of opiate. Never fear: These cookies will not induce sleep or dreams of poppy fields along yellow brick roads.

LEMON-BASIL BUTTER COOKIES

HANDS-ON 15 MIN. TOTAL 25 MIN.

Lemon and basil make a great pair in savory dishes, so we figured they'd marry well in a sweet cookie too. We were right. These delicate cookies have a refreshingly unique flavor that's worth sharing.

1. Preheat oven to 350°F. Process basil and ¼ cup sugar in a food processor until blended.

2. Beat butter at medium speed with an electric mixer until creamy; gradually add 1½ cups sugar, beating until blended. Add lemon juice and egg, beating until blended. Gradually add flour and basil mixture, beating until blended.

3. Shape dough into 1-inch balls; place 2 inches apart on lightly greased (with cooking spray) baking sheets. Flatten balls slightly with bottom of a glass dipped in remaining ¼ cup sugar.

4. Bake, in batches, at 350°F for 8 to 10 minutes or until lightly browned. Remove to wire racks, and cool completely (about 30 minutes).

*If you can't find lemon-basil, substitute regular fresh basil instead.

MAKES 6½ dozen

INGREDIENTS

1 cup fresh
lemon-basil leaves*

2 cups sugar, divided

1 lb. butter, softened

¼ cup fresh lemon juice

1 large egg

6 cups all-purpose
flour

Vegetable cooking spray

CINNAMON-ORANGE SQUARES

INGREDIENTS

1 cup butter, softened

¾ cup powdered sugar

2¼ cups all-purpose flour

¼ tsp. baking powder

⅛ tsp. table salt

2 Tbsp. loosely packed orange zest

1 tsp. ground cinnamon, divided

¼ tsp. ground nutmeg

Wax paper

Parchment paper

1 Tbsp. granulated sugar

HANDS-ON 30 MIN. TOTAL 2 HOURS, 40 MIN.

An uncommon pairing, orange and cinnamon go quite well together. These squares are a nice change of pace from the usual cookie rounds. Fill a cellophane sleeve with a stack of these and tie it with twine for the perfect hostess gift.

1. Beat butter at medium speed with an electric mixer until creamy. Gradually add powdered sugar, beating until blended.

2. Combine flour, baking powder, salt, orange zest, ¾ tsp. cinnamon, and nutmeg in a medium bowl. Gradually add flour mixture to butter mixture, beating at low speed until blended.

3. Divide dough into 2 equal portions; flatten each portion into a disk. Roll 1 portion of dough at a time to ¼-inch thickness between 2 sheets of wax paper. Transfer dough (in wax paper) to a baking sheet, and chill 1 hour.

4. Preheat oven to 350°F. Cut 1 portion of dough with a 2-inch square-shaped cutter, rerolling scraps once. Place 1 inch apart on parchment paper-lined baking sheets. Repeat procedure with remaining portion of dough.

5. Combine granulated sugar and remaining ¼ tsp. ground cinnamon in a small bowl; sprinkle mixture over cookies.

6. Bake, in batches, at 350°F for 12 to 14 minutes or until golden brown around edges. Cool on baking sheets 1 minute. Transfer to wire racks, and cool completely (about 30 minutes). Store in airtight containers.

MAKES 3 dozen

SAVORY BENNE WAFERS

Hands-on 30 min. Total 2 hours, 35 min.

South Carolina's culinary duo, the Lee brothers, have turned traditional sweet benne wafers, a Lowcountry staple, into these savory, one-bite cocktail snacks. Benne, aka sesame, seeds can be found in large jars in the Asian food aisle and at health food stores.

1. Preheat oven to 325°F. Cook benne seeds in a heavy skillet over medium heat, stirring often, 6 to 7 minutes or until browned and fragrant. (Seeds will be the color of pecans.) Transfer to a plate; and cool completely (about 20 minutes).

2. Process flour, next 2 ingredients, and 1 Tbsp. seeds in a food processor 30 seconds or until seeds are finely ground. (Seeds should be the same consistency as flour.) Add butter; pulse 5 or 6 times or until mixture is crumbly and resembles small peas. Add half of ice-cold water, 1 Tbsp. at a time, and pulse 2 or 3 times or until just combined. Add 1 Tbsp. sesame seeds and remaining water; process 10 to 15 seconds or until dough forms a ball and pulls away from sides of bowl.

3. Divide dough into 4 equal portions on a lightly floured surface; dust tops of dough with flour. Roll each portion of dough to $\frac{1}{16}$-inch thickness on a lightly floured surface. Sprinkle 1 portion of dough with 2 tsp. benne seeds; roll gently to press seeds into dough. Cut dough with a 2-inch round-shaped cutter; place $\frac{1}{2}$ inch apart on parchment paper-lined baking sheets. Repeat procedure with remaining dough and sesame seeds.

4. Bake, in batches, at 325°F for 23 to 25 minutes or until lightly browned. Transfer baking sheets to wire racks, and cool completely (about 20 minutes). Store in an airtight container up to 3 days.

MAKES about 6 dozen

INGREDIENTS

¼ cup plus 2 tsp. benne (sesame) seeds

2 cups all-purpose flour

1½ tsp. kosher salt

¼ tsp. ground red pepper

¾ cup cold unsalted butter, cut into small pieces

¼ cup ice-cold water

Parchment paper

CORNMEAL SUGAR COOKIES

INGREDIENTS

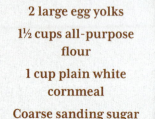

1 cup butter, softened

1 cup granulated sugar

2 large egg yolks

1½ cups all-purpose flour

1 cup plain white cornmeal

Coarse sanding sugar

Parchment paper

HANDS-ON 10 MIN. TOTAL 30 MIN.

Cornmeal lends a Southern note and a complex crunch to traditional sugar cookies. Cut the dough into desired shapes for added interest.

1. Preheat oven to 300°F. Beat butter and granulated sugar at medium speed with a heavy-duty electric stand mixer until creamy. Add egg yolks, 1 at a time, beating until blended after each addition.

2. Combine flour and cornmeal in a medium bowl. Gradually add flour mixture to butter mixture, beating until just blended.

3. Roll dough to ¼-inch thickness on a well-floured surface. Cut with a diamond-shaped cutter; sprinkle with sanding sugar. Place 2 inches apart on parchment paper-lined baking sheets.

4. Bake, in batches, at 300°F for 14 to 16 minutes or until lightly browned. Transfer to wire racks, and cool completely (about 20 minutes).

MAKES about 3½ dozen

SMART COOKIE

What's in a name? Cornmeal, grits, polenta, masa, white or yellow cornmeal mix, stone-ground or instant . . . it can be confusing. Cornmeal typically refers to a finer ground meal than grits or polenta. For best quality, stick to cornmeal that is stone-ground, and choose yellow or white to suit your preference. Stick to classic cornmeal (not mix) for this recipe.

CRUNCHY LACE COOKIES

HANDS-ON 8 MIN. TOTAL 35 MIN.

Lace cookies get their name from the tiny perforations that form in the dough as they bake. The lacelike effect creates a delicate, crisp cookie that's an elegant addition to a cookie tray and perfect for teatime.

1. Preheat oven to 350°F. Stir together 2 Tbsp. hot water and baking soda in a large bowl until baking soda is dissolved. Add butter and corn syrup, stirring until blended.

2. Combine oats and next 3 ingredients in a medium bowl; add oat mixture to butter mixture, stirring until blended.

3. Shape dough into ¾-inch balls; place 3 inches apart, on lightly greased (with cooking spray) baking sheets; flatten dough slightly with hand.

4. Bake, in batches, at 350°F for 7 to 8 minutes or until golden brown. Transfer to wire racks, and cool completely (about 20 minutes).

MAKES 2 dozen

INGREDIENTS

2 Tbsp. hot water

1½ tsp. baking soda

¾ cup butter, melted

1 Tbsp. light corn syrup

1½ cups uncooked regular oats

1½ cups firmly packed light brown sugar

1½ cups all-purpose flour

1½ cups sweetened flaked coconut

Vegetable cooking spray

INGREDIENTS

1 cup butter, softened

½ cup sugar

2½ cups all-purpose flour

⅓ cup toasted finely chopped pecans

1 tsp. vanilla extract

Parchment paper

PECAN SANDIES

HANDS-ON 10 MIN. TOTAL 3 HOURS

Cookies made with fresh Texas pecans are a cookie jar staple in the Lone Star state. Good thing batches are bigger in Texas, too, because you can't eat just one of these. This cookie gets its name from its very fine crumbly texture.

1. Beat butter and sugar at medium speed with an electric mixer until fluffy; gradually add flour, beating just until blended. Add pecans and vanilla, beating until blended.

2. Divide dough into 2 equal portions. Shape each into 2 (1¼-inch-thick) logs (about 12 inches long). Wrap each in parchment paper, and chill 1 hour or until firm.

3. Preheat oven to 325°F. Cut each log into ¼-inch-thick slices; place ½ inch apart on parchment paper-lined baking sheets.

4. Bake, in batches, at 325°F for 18 to 20 minutes or until lightly browned. Cool on baking sheets 5 minutes. Transfer to wire racks, and cool completely (about 20 minutes).

MAKES about 7 dozen

ALMOND SNOWBALLS

HANDS-ON 10 MIN. TOTAL 1 HOUR, 40 MIN.

The South might sing, "Let it snow!" but only very rarely is much of the region graced with a dusting of the stuff. Maybe that's what makes these snowy cookies so appealing. Roll these almond balls in the powdered sugar after they've cooled but are still warm.

1. Preheat oven to 325°F. Process almonds in a food processor 30 seconds or until very finely ground.

2. Beat butter at medium speed with a heavy-duty electric stand mixer until creamy. Gradually add vanilla and 1 cup powdered sugar, beating until blended. (Dough will be crumbly.)

3. Combine flour, salt, and almonds in a medium bowl; gradually add flour mixture to butter mixture, beating until blended

4. Shape dough into ¾-inch balls; place 2 inches apart on parchment paper-lined baking sheets.

5. Bake, in batches, at 325°F for 12 to 15 minutes or until lightly browned around edges. Cool on baking sheets 2 minutes. Transfer to wire racks, and cool 10 minutes. Roll warm cookies in remaining ½ cup powdered sugar.

MAKES about 5 dozen

★ PARTY PERFECT

Dress up these almond cookies with different coatings like cocoa, cinnamon sugar, or powdered chai tea mix to add interest to a cookie plate. You can also spike the powdered sugar with a flavorful dose of ground clove, allspice, nutmeg, or ginger.

INGREDIENTS

½ cup toasted slivered almonds

1 cup butter, softened

1 tsp. vanilla extract

1½ cups powdered sugar, divided

2½ cups all-purpose flour

¼ tsp. table salt

Parchment paper

SNICKERDOODLES

HANDS-ON 10 MIN. TOTAL 1 HOUR, 30 MIN.

Distinguished by a cracked cinnamon-sugar surface, Snickerdoodles are leavened with baking powder, which gives them their characteristic plumpness and tender crumb.

1. Preheat oven to 375°F. Beat butter at medium speed with an electric mixer until creamy. Gradually add 2 cups sugar, beating until blended. Add eggs, milk, and vanilla, beating until blended.

2. Combine flour, baking powder, and 2 tsp. cinnamon in a large bowl; gradually add flour mixture to butter mixture, beating at low speed just until blended. (If desired, refrigerate in an airtight container up to 1 week.)

3. Combine remaining 3 Tbsp. sugar and remaining 1½ Tbsp. cinnamon in a small bowl. Roll dough into 1¼-inch balls; roll in cinnamon-sugar. Place on ungreased baking sheets; flatten dough slightly with hand.

4. Bake, in batches, at 375°F for 11 to 13 minutes or until lightly browned. Cool on baking sheets 5 minutes. Transfer to wire racks, and cool completely (about 30 minutes).

MAKES 4½ dozen

INGREDIENTS

1 cup butter, softened

2 cups plus 3 Tbsp. sugar

2 large eggs

¼ cup milk

1 tsp. vanilla extract

3¾ cups all-purpose flour

1 tsp. baking powder

2 Tbsp. plus ½ tsp. ground cinnamon

SMART COOKIE

If the nonsensical name of these cookies makes you smile, know it's most likely a corruption of the German schneckennudeln, or "snail noodles," a sweet pastry dough sprinkled with cinnamon-sugar, formed into a spiral, and baked to create a swirly cinnamon roll reminiscent of a snail's shell (and the flavor profile of a snickerdoodle).

CLASSIC SUGAR COOKIES

Hands-on 25 min. Total 1 hour, 35 min.

This dough is the perfect cookie canvas for cutting into seasonal shapes, decorating with icing, or smearing with frosting, and finishing with sprinkles.

1. Beat butter at medium speed with an electric mixer until creamy; gradually add granulated sugar, beating until blended. Add egg and vanilla, beating until blended.

2. Combine flour and salt in a medium bowl. Gradually add flour mixture to butter mixture, beating until blended. Divide dough into 2 equal portions. Wrap each portion in plastic, and chill 1 hour.

3. Preheat oven to 350°F. Roll each portion of dough to ¼-inch thickness on a lightly floured surface. Cut dough with desired cookie cutters. Place on lightly greased (with cooking spray) baking sheets.

4. Bake, in batches, at 350°F for 8 to 10 minutes or until lightly browned around edges. Cool on baking sheets 1 minute. Transfer to wire racks, and cool completely (about 30 minutes).

5. Dip cookies in Glaze, and sprinkle immediately with sanding sugar. Let stand 30 minutes or until set.

MAKES about 1¾ dozen

GLAZE

Whisk together **1 (16-oz.) package powdered sugar** and **6 Tbsp. warm water** until smooth. Divide mixture, and tint with **food coloring,** if desired. (Place in shallow bowls for ease in dipping cookies.)

INGREDIENTS

1 cup butter, softened

1 cup granulated sugar

1 large egg

1 tsp. vanilla extract

3 cups all-purpose flour

¼ tsp. table salt

Vegetable cooking spray

Glaze

1 (3.25-oz.) jar coarse sanding sugar

DATE PINWHEELS

INGREDIENTS

1 (10-oz.) package chopped dates

¾ cup granulated sugar, divided

¼ tsp. table salt, divided

1 cup chopped walnuts

½ cup butter, softened

½ cup firmly packed brown sugar

1 large egg

½ tsp. vanilla extract

2 cups all-purpose flour

¼ tsp. baking soda

Wax paper

Parchment paper

HANDS-ON 30 MIN. TOTAL 1 HOUR, 45 MIN.

Sweet chopped dates and crunchy walnuts rolled into cookie dough and sliced into pinwheels make a cookie that's as pretty as it is tasty. Make these ahead and freeze for later, or serve them warm, straight from the oven.

1. Combine dates, ¼ cup granulated sugar, ½ cup water, and ⅛ tsp. salt in a medium saucepan over medium-high heat. Bring mixture to a boil; reduce heat, and simmer 3 to 5 minutes. Remove from heat; stir in walnuts, and set aside.

2. Beat butter, remaining ½ cup granulated sugar, and brown sugar at medium speed with an electric mixer until fluffy. Add egg and vanilla, beating until blended. Gradually add remaining ⅛ tsp. salt, flour, and baking soda, beating until blended. Cover and chill 1 hour.

3. Preheat oven to 375°F. Roll dough into an 18- x 12-inch rectangle on lightly floured wax paper. Spread date mixture evenly over dough, leaving a ½-inch border.

4. Roll cookie dough up, jelly-roll fashion, starting at long side; wrap dough in wax paper, and chill 1 hour.

5. Cut dough into ¼-inch-thick slices; place on parchment paper-lined baking sheets.

6. Bake, in batches, at 375°F for 12 to 14 minutes or until lightly browned. Cool on baking sheets 2 to 3 minutes. Transfer to wire racks, and cool completely (about 30 minutes).

MAKES 2½ dozen

CHOCOLATE-ORANGE SWIRLS

HANDS-ON 25 MIN. TOTAL 2 HOURS, 40 MIN.

Fresh zest accentuates the orange flavor in these memorable cookies that are fun to make.

1. Beat butter at medium speed with an electric mixer until creamy; gradually add sugar, beating until blended. Add egg and vanilla; beating until blended.

2. Combine flour, baking powder, and salt in a medium bowl; gradually add flour mixture to butter mixture, beating at low speed until blended.

3. Remove half of dough from bowl. Add orange zest and orange extract to portion of dough in bowl, beating until blended. Remove dough from bowl, and set aside. Place remaining dough portion in mixing bowl; add melted chocolate, beating until blended. Cover and chill both portions of dough 1 hour.

4. Roll orange dough portion into a 15- x 8-inch rectangle on floured wax paper. Invert orange dough onto chocolate dough; peel off wax paper, and press orange dough firmly onto chocolate dough with a rolling pin.

5. Roll cookie dough up, jelly-roll fashion, starting at short side; wrap dough in wax paper, and chill 1 hour.

6. Cut dough into ¼-inch slices; place on ungreased baking sheets.

7. Bake, in batches, at 350°F for 10 to 12 minutes. Transfer to wire racks, and cool completely (about 30 minutes).

NOTE: To prevent flat-sided cookies, turn dough rolls halfway through the second chilling time. Dental floss makes cutting the dough easier.

MAKES 2½ dozen

INGREDIENTS

1 cup butter, softened

1 cup sugar

1 large egg

1 tsp. vanilla extract

3 cups all-purpose flour

1½ tsp. baking powder

¼ tsp. salt

1 tsp. loosely packed orange zest

1½ tsp. orange extract

2 (1-oz.) squares semisweet chocolate, melted and cooled

Wax paper

SLICE-AND-BAKE SHORTBREAD COOKIES

INGREDIENTS

1 cup butter, softened

¾ cup powdered sugar

2 tsp. vanilla extract

½ tsp. almond extract

2 cups all-purpose flour

¼ tsp. baking powder

⅛ tsp. table salt

Wax paper

Parchment paper

HANDS-ON 15 MIN. TOTAL 5 HOURS, 15 MIN.

Keep logs of this dough in your freezer to bake up when company's coming or unexpected guests arrive.

1. Beat butter at medium speed with an electric mixer until creamy; gradually add powdered sugar, beating until smooth. Add vanilla and almond extract, beating until blended.

2. Combine flour, baking powder, and salt in a medium bowl; gradually add flour mixture to butter mixture, beating at low speed until blended.

3. Roll dough into 2 (7-inch) logs. Wrap each in wax paper, and chill 4 hours, or freeze in zip-top plastic freezer bags up to 1 month.

4. Preheat oven to 350°F. If frozen, let logs stand at room temperature 10 minutes. Cut each log into 24 slices; place shortbread slices 1 inch apart on parchment paper-lined baking sheets.

5. Bake, in batches, at 350°F for 10 to 12 minutes or until lightly browned around edges. Transfer to wire racks, and let cool completely (about 20 minutes). Store in airtight containers.

MAKES 4 dozen

COOKIE SWAP

For Coconut-Macadamia Nut Shortbread Cookies, omit almond extract. Stir in 1 cup toasted coconut, ½ cup finely chopped macadamia nuts, and ¼ tsp. coconut extract with vanilla in Step 1.

BROWNED BUTTER-PECAN SHORTBREAD

Hands-on 30 min. Total 5 hours, 50 min.

These rich-tasting pecan shortbread cookies are not overly sweet and are a great addition to a holiday appetizer and dessert buffet. The amount of butter in the cookies makes them crumble easily, so be careful when arranging them on the platter. If you have some cookies that crumble, just use the crumbs as a delicious topping for ice cream.

1. Cook butter in a small heavy saucepan over medium heat, stirring constantly, 6 to 8 minutes or until butter begins to turn golden brown. Remove pan immediately from heat, and pour butter into a small bowl. Cover and chill 1 hour or until butter is cool and begins to solidify.

2. Beat butter at medium speed with an electric mixer until creamy; gradually add brown sugar and powdered sugar, beating until smooth. Gradually add flour to butter mixture, beating at low speed just until blended. Stir in chopped pecans.

3. Shape dough into 4 (8-inch) logs. Wrap logs tightly in plastic, and chill 4 hours or until firm.

4. Preheat oven to 350°F. Cut each log into ¼-inch-thick slices; place on lightly greased (with cooking spray) baking sheets. Press 1 pecan half into each slice.

5. Bake, in batches, at 350°F for 8 to 10 minutes or until lightly browned. Transfer to wire racks, and cool completely (about 30 minutes).

MAKES about 10½ dozen

INGREDIENTS

1½ cups butter

¾ cup firmly packed brown sugar

¾ cup powdered sugar

3 cups all-purpose flour

1½ cups toasted chopped pecans

Vegetable cooking spray

CHEWY COFFEE-TOFFEE SHORTBREAD

HANDS-ON 15 MIN. TOTAL 1 HOUR, 40 MIN.

Toffee bits give this golden shortbread its slightly chewy texture. This cookie is particularly nice dipped in a cup of coffee.

INGREDIENTS

1 cup butter, softened

½ cup firmly packed light brown sugar

1 Tbsp. instant espresso powder

1 Tbsp. hot water

2¼ cups all-purpose flour

⅛ tsp. table salt

½ cup almond toffee bits

1. Beat butter at medium speed with an electric mixer until creamy; gradually add sugar, beating until blended. Stir together espresso powder and 1 Tbsp. hot water. Add to butter mixture, stirring until blended.

2. Combine flour and salt in a medium bowl; gradually add flour mixture to butter mixture, beating at low speed until blended. Stir in toffee bits. Cover and chill 30 minutes.

3. Prehat oven to 275°F. Roll dough to ½-inch thickness on a lightly floured surface. Cut dough with fluted rectangular cutters; place 2 inches apart on ungreased baking sheets.

4. Bake at 275°F for 50 minutes. Cool 2 minutes on baking sheets. Transfer to wire racks, and cool completely (about 20 minutes).

NOTE: If you can't find almond toffee bits in the supermarket, substitute ½ cup finely crushed Skor candy bars or crushed Werther's Original candies.

MAKES 2 dozen

DARK CHOCOLATE-ESPRESSO SHORTBREAD

Hands-on 35 min. Total 1 hour

Edges tipped with unsweetened chocolate and white chocolate enhance the coffee flavor in these delightful, dunkable cookies.

1. Preheat oven to 325°F. Beat butter at medium speed with an electric mixer until fluffy; gradually add powdered sugar, beating until blended.

2. Combine flour and next 4 ingredients in a medium bowl; gradually add flour mixture to butter mixture, beating just until blended.

3. Divide dough into 3 equal portions; place on parchment paper-lined baking sheets.

4. Cover dough portions with plastic wrap; gently press or roll each portion of dough into a 5½-inch circle. Lightly score each with a sharp knife into 6 or 8 wedges.

5. Bake at 325°F for 23 minutes or until shortbread feels firm to the touch. Gently score each round again with a sharp knife. Transfer rounds (on parchment paper) to wire racks, and cool completely (about 30 minutes). Cut shortbread into wedges along scored lines.

6. Microwave white chocolate and unsweetened chocolate in separate microwave-safe bowls at HIGH 1 minute, or until melted and smooth, stirring after 30 seconds. Partially dip wide end of each shortbread wedge in unsweetened chocolate. Place on a wax paper-lined jelly-roll pan, and freeze briefly to set chocolate. Partially dip other half of wide end of each wedge in white chocolate. Drizzle white chocolate over unsweetened chocolate-dipped end. Freeze briefly to set white chocolate.

MAKES 1½ to 2 dozen

INGREDIENTS

1 cup unsalted butter, softened

1 cup powdered sugar

1¼ cups all-purpose flour

¼ cup cornstarch

¼ cup unsweetened cocoa

1 tsp. instant espresso powder

¼ tsp. table salt

Parchment paper

1 (4-oz.) white chocolate baking bar

1 (4-oz.) unsweetened chocolate baking bars

Wax paper

GINGER-OATMEAL-SORGHUM COOKIES

INGREDIENTS

4 cups all-purpose flour

1 Tbsp. baking soda

1½ tsp. table salt

4 cups uncooked quick-cooking oats

1½ cups raisins

1¾ cups sugar, divided

1½ tsp. ground ginger

1 cup butter, melted

1 cup sorghum syrup

1 cup chopped walnuts

2 Tbsp. hot water

2 large eggs, lightly beaten

Vegetable cooking spray

HANDS-ON 20 MIN. TOTAL 50 MIN.

Sorghum, the South's most deeply flavored syrup, connects us to our culinary past and offers untapped potential to make everything more delicious. These cookies are absolutely no exception.

1. Preheat oven to 375°F. Combine flour, baking soda, salt, oats, raisins, 1¼ cups sugar, and ginger in a large bowl; add butter and next 4 ingredients, stirring until blended.

2. Shape dough into 20 (2-inch) balls; place 2 inches apart on lightly greased (with cooking spray) baking sheets. Flatten each ball to ¼-inch thickness. Brush tops with 1 to 2 Tbsp. water, and sprinkle evenly with remaining ½ cup sugar.

3. Bake at 375°F for 10 to 12 minutes or until lightly browned. Transfer to wire racks, and cool completely (about 20 minutes).

MAKES 1¾ dozen

BOURBON-PECAN-GINGERBREAD COOKIES

Hands-on 20 min. Total 13 hours, 30 min.

Be sure to bake the dough while cold. Otherwise, it will spread too much, and the cookies will lose their light, fluffy texture.

1. Combine first 8 ingredients in a large bowl. Combine ground pecans and next 7 ingredients in a second bowl. Add pecan mixture to flour mixture, stirring until smooth. Cover and chill 12 hours.

2. Preheat oven to 350°F. Drop dough by level spoonfuls 2 inches apart onto 2 parchment paper-lined baking sheets, using a 2-oz. ice-cream scoop (about 2 Tbsp.). Place 3 pecans on each cookie.

3. Bake, in batches, at 350°F for 15 to 18 minutes or until lightly browned around edges. Cool on baking sheets 5 minutes. Transfer to wire racks; cool completely (about 30 minutes). Drizzle with Bourbon Glaze.

MAKES about 2 dozen

BOURBON GLAZE

Whisk together **6 Tbsp. bourbon** and **3 cups powdered sugar** in a small bowl until smooth. Stir in water, 1 tsp. at a time, until the desired consistency.

INGREDIENTS

4 cups all-purpose flour

2 tsp. kosher salt

2 tsp. ground cinnamon

2 tsp. ground ginger

1 tsp. baking soda

½ tsp. ground cloves

½ tsp. ground allspice

½ tsp. ground nutmeg

4 cups finely ground toasted pecans

2 cups firmly packed dark brown sugar

½ cup bourbon

½ cup buttermilk

2 Tbsp. molasses

6 large eggs, lightly beaten

1 Tbsp. loosely packed lemon zest

1 Tbsp. loosely packed orange zest

Parchment paper

2 cups toasted pecan halves

Bourbon Glaze

MOLASSES-SPICE CRINKLES

Hands-on 15 min. Total 1 hour, 30 min.

For centuries, Southerners have treasured their jars of molasses—the cooked-down sugarcane mixture that is thick, brown, sticky, and sharp with tangy sweetness. From the hills of Tennessee to the plains of Georgia, the syrup is a table condiment for drizzling on biscuits and pancakes or stirring into desserts. The strong, sweet flavor of molasses balances well with a team of spices in these soft, chewy cookies encrusted with sugar.

1. Preheat oven to 375°F. Beat shortening at medium speed with an electric mixer until fluffy; gradually add 1 cup granulated sugar, beating until blended. Add egg and molasses, beating until blended.

2. Combine flour and next 8 ingredients in a medium bowl. Add flour mixture to shortening mixture in 4 additions, beating at low speed after each addition until blended. Cover and chill 1 hour.

3. Shape dough into 1-inch balls, and roll in sanding sugar; place 2 inches apart on ungreased baking sheets.

4. Bake, in batches, at 375°F for 9 to 11 minutes. (Tops will crack.) Transfer to wire racks, and cool completely (about 30 minutes).

MAKES 3 dozen

INGREDIENTS

¾ cup shortening

1 cup granulated sugar

1 large egg

¼ cup molasses

2 cups all-purpose flour

1 tsp. baking powder

1 tsp. baking soda

¼ tsp. table salt

1 tsp. ground ginger

1 tsp. ground cinnamon

½ tsp. ground nutmeg

¼ tsp. ground cloves

¼ tsp. ground allspice

1 cup sanding sugar

⭐ PARTY PERFECT

For a fun twist, roll the dough balls in colored sanding sugar for crinkles in sparkling hues to fit your occasion.

EASIEST PEANUT BUTTER COOKIES

Hands-on 20 min. Total 1 hour, 5 min.

Impress your guests (and your taste buds) with these simple, four-ingredient peanut butter cookies. That signature peanut butter cookie cross-hatch pattern is created with the tines of a fork.

1. Preheat oven to 325°F. Beat all ingredients in a large bowl until combined.

2. Shape dough into 1-inch balls; place balls 1 inch apart on ungreased baking sheets. Flatten slightly with tines of a fork.

3. Bake at 325°F for 15 minutes or until golden brown. Transfer to wire racks, and cool completely (about 20 minutes).

MAKES about 2½ dozen

COOKIE SWAP

Peanut Butter-and-Chocolate Cookies: Divide peanut butter cookie dough in half. Stir 2 melted semisweet chocolate baking squares into half of dough. Shape doughs into 30 (1-inch) half peanut butter, half chocolate-peanut butter balls. Flatten slightly with tines of a fork. Proceed with recipe as directed.

INGREDIENTS

1 cup peanut butter

1 cup sugar

1 large egg

1 tsp. vanilla extract

CANDY BAR-PEANUT BUTTER COOKIES

INGREDIENTS

1 cup butter, softened

1 cup granulated sugar

1 cup firmly packed brown sugar

1 cup creamy peanut butter

2 large eggs

1 tsp. vanilla extract

2 cups all-purpose flour

1 tsp. baking soda

½ tsp. table salt

36 bite-size chocolate-covered caramel-peanut nougat bars

Parchment paper

Hands-on 30 min. Total 1 hour, 50 min.

Substitute your favorite gooey chocolate candy bar to change things up.

1. Beat first 4 ingredients at medium speed with an electric mixer until smooth. Add eggs and vanilla; beating until blended.

2. Combine flour and next 2 ingredients in a small bowl. Add flour mixture to butter mixture, beating until blended. Cover and chill 30 minutes.

3. Preheat oven to 350°F. Shape about 2 Tbsp. dough around each nougat bar, using lightly floured hands, covering completely, to form balls; place 3 inches apart on parchment paper-lined baking sheets.

4. Bake, in batches, at 350°F for 13 to 14 minutes or until lightly browned. Cool on baking sheets 5 minutes. Transfer to wire racks, and cool completely (about 30 minutes).

NOTE: We tested with Snickers Minis.

MAKES 3 dozen

GRITSCOTTI

Hands-on 30 min. Total 3 hours

Grits + biscotti = Gritscotti. Deep South and Old World collide in this rustic, givable sweet. After baking the logs, gently cut them with a serrated knife for even slices. If you break a few slices, bake them anyway, and sprinkle the bits over yogurt for a flavorful breakfast treat.

1. Preheat oven to 325°F. Beat butter, sugar and zest at medium speed with an electric mixer until creamy. Add eggs, 1 at a time, beating until blended after each addition.

2. Combine flour, grits, baking powder, and salt. Add flour mixture and cranberries to butter mixture, beating at low speed just until blended.

3. Divide dough into 3 equal portions. Lightly flour hands, and shape each portion into a 12½- x 9-inch slightly flattened log; place about 2 inches apart on a parchment paper-lined baking sheet.

4. Bake at 325°F for 30 to 35 minutes or until lightly browned. Transfer to wire racks, and cool 15 minutes. Reduce oven temperature to 300°F.

5. Cut each log into ¼- to ½-inch-thick slices with a serrated knife using a gentle sawing motion; place slices on 3 parchment paper-lined baking sheets.

6. Bake, in batches, at 300°F for 30 to 35 minutes or until golden brown. Cool on baking sheets 10 minutes. Transfer cookies (on parchment paper) to wire racks, and cool completely (about 30 minutes).

MAKES about 4 dozen

INGREDIENTS

¾ cup butter, softened

1½ cups sugar

1 Tbsp. loosely packed orange zest

4 large eggs

3 cups all-purpose flour

1½ cups instant grits

1 Tbsp. baking powder

1 tsp. kosher salt

1½ cups sweetened dried cranberries

Parchment paper

PEPPERMINT WEDDING COOKIES

Hands-on 20 min. Total 1 hour, 40 min.

This recipe tastes like a hybrid of a wedding cookie and a meltaway mint. The peppermint candy crumbs add a burst of refreshing sweetness to each bite.

INGREDIENTS

1 cup powdered sugar, divided

1 cup unsalted butter, softened

1 tsp. peppermint extract

2 cups all-purpose flour

½ tsp. table salt

10 hard peppermint candies, crushed

Parchment paper

1. Sift ½ cup powdered sugar. Beat butter at medium speed with an electric mixer until creamy; gradually add sifted powdered sugar and peppermint extract, beating until blended. Add flour and salt, beating until blended. Cover and chill 30 minutes.

2. Preheat oven to 350°F. Place crushed peppermints in a bowl. Place remaining ½ cup powdered sugar in a second bowl. Shape dough into 20 (1¼-inch) balls; place 1 inch apart on parchment paper-lined baking sheets.

3. Bake, in batches, at 350°F for 18 minutes or until bottoms are golden brown (tops will be pale). Immediately roll each cookie in crushed peppermints and then in remaining powdered sugar. Generously sprinkle crushed peppermints on top of each cookie, mounding slightly. (Peppermints will stick to cookies as they cool.) Transfer baking sheets to wire racks, and cool completely (about 30 minutes).

MAKES 1½ dozen

PARTY PERFECT

Look for green-and-white swirled peppermints or even multi-colored candy canes to add more pizzazz.

BARS AND BROWNIES

THE SCOOP ON PERFECT BARS AND BROWNIES

Keep these tricks in your back pocket for the best hand-held treats, bar none.

1. A pan and a plan ensures bar and brownie perfection. Choose precisely.

2. Line pans with foil, then grease with shortening for easy cleanup.

3. A bench or pastry scraper makes cutting easy. Use a pizza cutter or chef's knife too.

4. Use the foil liner to lift out the brownies or bars with ease.

PEACH MELBA SHORTBREAD BARS

Hands-on 20 min. Total 2 hours, 20 min.

The father of French cooking, Auguste Escoffier, created the classic peach Melba—fresh peaches and raspberry sauce over vanilla ice cream—at London's Savoy Hotel for the soprano Nellie Melba. All the goodness that made the dish famous is in these delicious bars. They're even better made with homemade preserves from Southern peaches.

1. Preheat oven to 350°F. Combine first 3 ingredients in a medium bowl. Cut butter into flour mixture with a pastry blender or fork until crumbly. Reserve 1 cup flour mixture. Press remaining flour mixture onto bottom of a lightly greased (with cooking spray) 11- x 7-inch or 9-inch square pan.

2. Bake at 350°F for 25 to 30 minutes or until lightly browned.

3. Spread peach preserves over crust in pan. Dollop raspberry preserves by ½ teaspoonfuls over peach preserves. Sprinkle reserved 1 cup flour mixture over preserves. Sprinkle with sliced almonds.

4. Bake at 350°F for 35 to 40 minutes or until golden brown. Cool in pan 1 hour on a wire rack. Cut into bars.

MAKES about 1½ to 2 dozen bars

INGREDIENTS

2 cups all-purpose flour

½ cup sugar

¼ tsp. table salt

1 cup cold butter

Vegetable cooking spray

1 cup peach preserves

6 tsp. raspberry preserves

½ cup sliced almonds

Garnish: sweetened whipped cream

BLACKBERRY-PEACH COBBLER BARS

INGREDIENTS

1 cup butter, softened

1 cup firmly packed light brown sugar

1½ cups granulated sugar, divided

4 large eggs

1 Tbsp. vanilla extract

1 tsp. baking powder

¾ tsp. table salt

3¼ cups all-purpose flour, divided

Shortening

3 (6-oz.) packages fresh blackberries (about 4 cups)

4 cups peeled and sliced fresh firm, ripe peaches

3 Tbsp. bourbon

1 cup sliced almonds

Hands-on 20 min. Total 2 hours, 20 min.

Toasted sliced almonds add a streusel-like crunch to the tops of these Southern bramble-meets-orchard bars.

1. Preheat oven to 350°F. Beat first 2 ingredients and 1 cup granulated sugar at medium speed with an electric mixer until creamy. Add eggs, 1 at a time, beating just until blended after each addition. Stir in vanilla.

2. Combine baking powder, salt, and 3 cups flour in a medium bowl; gradually add flour mixture to butter mixture, beating just until blended. Spread three-fourths of batter in a greased (with shortening) and floured 13- x 9-inch pan; sprinkle with blackberries.

3. Combine remaining ½ cup granulated sugar and ¼ cup flour in a medium bowl; add peaches and bourbon, stirring to coat. Spoon mixture over blackberries. Dollop remaining one-fourth batter over peach mixture; sprinkle with almonds.

4. Bake at 350°F for 1 hour or until golden brown and bubbly. Cool completely in pan on a wire rack (about 1 hour). Cut into bars.

MAKES about 1 dozen bars

STRAWBERRY-LEMON SHORTBREAD BARS

HANDS-ON 20 MIN. TOTAL 8 HOURS, 10 MIN.

Sweet strawberries brightened by the sunny freshness of tart lemon are a classic dessert pairing. Now you can enjoy the combo in these pretty chilled bars. Refrigerate leftovers, stored in an airtight container, up to two days.

1. Preheat oven to 350°F. Combine flour, powdered sugar, and ½ tsp. lemon zest in a medium bowl; cut in butter with a pastry blender until crumbly. Press mixture onto bottom of a lightly greased (with cooking spray) 13- x 9-inch pan.

2. Bake at 350°F for 20 to 22 minutes or until lightly browned.

3. Meanwhile, beat cream cheese and granulated sugar with an electric mixer until smooth. Add eggs, 1 at a time, beating just until blended after each addition. Stir in fresh lemon juice and remaining ¼ tsp. lemon zest, beating until blended.

4. Spread preserves over crust. Pour cream cheese mixture over preserves, spreading to edges. Bake 28 to 32 more minutes or until set. Cool in pan 1 hour on a wire rack; cover and chill 4 to 8 hours. Cut into bars.

MAKES 4 dozen bars

INGREDIENTS

2 cups all-purpose flour

½ cup powdered sugar

¾ tsp. loosely packed lemon zest, divided

¾ cup cold butter

Vegetable cooking spray

2 (8-oz.) packages cream cheese, softened

¾ cup granulated sugar

2 large eggs

1 Tbsp. fresh lemon juice

1 cup strawberry preserves

ORANGE DREAMSICLE CRISPY TREATS

These no-bake treats are a gussied-up classic. You can also use yellow and pink food coloring gel to make peach. Practice on a piece of wax paper, adding a little at a time to achieve the perfect shade.

1. Melt ¼ cup butter in a large Dutch oven over medium-low heat; cook 2 minutes, or until butter is melted. Add marshmallows; cook, stirring constantly, 3 minutes or until melted. Remove from heat.

2. Stir in 1½ tsp. vanilla. Add orange cake mix, stirring until blended. Add cereal and white chocolate morsels, stirring until well coated. Spread mixture into a lightly greased (with cooking spray) 13- x 9-inch pan. Cool completely (about 30 minutes).

3. Meanwhile, stir together powdered sugar, remaining 6 Tbsp. butter, orange juice, remaining ¼ tsp. vanilla extract, orange extract, and desired amount of peach food coloring gel. Spread over cereal mixture. Let stand 1 hour before cutting into bars.

NOTE: We tested with Duncan Hines Orange Supreme cake mix.

MAKES 32 bars

INGREDIENTS

¼ cup plus 6 Tbsp. butter, softened, divided

1 (10-oz.) package miniature marshmallows

1¾ tsp. vanilla extract, divided

½ cup orange cake mix

6 cups crisp rice cereal

1 (12-oz.) package white chocolate morsels

Vegetable cooking spray

3 cups powdered sugar

6 Tbsp. fresh orange juice

¼ tsp. orange extract

Peach food coloring gel

LEMON-ALMOND BARS

HANDS-ON 30 MIN. TOTAL 2 HOURS, 35 MIN.

The classic tart lemon bar gets a nutty flavor and crunch with the addition of sliced almonds. Pecans would make a decidedly Southern stand-in.

1. Preheat oven to 350°F. Beat ¼ cup granulated sugar, ¾ cup softened butter, and 1 tsp. zest at medium speed with a heavy-duty electric stand mixer 2 minutes or until creamy.

2. Combine 2 cups flour and ¼ tsp. salt in a medium bowl. Gradually add flour mixture to butter mixture, beating just until blended. Press dough into bottom of a lightly greased (with cooking spray) 13- x 9-inch baking pan. Chill 15 minutes.

3. Bake at 350°F for 15 to 20 minutes or until lightly browned. Remove from oven; reduce oven temperature to 325°F.

4. Whisk together eggs and 2 cups sugar. Process ginger and ½ cup flour in a food processor 1 minute or until ginger is finely chopped. Stir in baking powder. Whisk ginger mixture into egg mixture. Whisk in lemon juice and remaining 2 Tbsp. lemon zest; pour over crust.

5. Bake at 325°F for 15 to 20 minutes or until filling is just set. Remove from oven.

6. Combine remaining ¾ cup flour, ½ cup sugar, and ¼ tsp. salt in a small bowl. Microwave remaining ¼ cup butter in a microwave-safe bowl at HIGH 10 seconds or until melted; add to flour mixture, stirring until blended. Stir in almonds. Sprinkle over hot lemon mixture, and bake 20 to 25 more minutes or just until lightly browned. Cool completely in pan on a wire rack (about 1 hour). Cut into squares.

MAKES 32 bars

INGREDIENTS

2¾ cups sugar, divided

1 cup butter, softened, divided

2 Tbsp. plus 1 tsp. loosely packed lemon zest, divided

3¼ cups all-purpose flour, divided

½ tsp. table salt, divided

Vegetable cooking spray

6 large eggs

¼ cup chopped crystallized ginger

1 tsp. baking powder

⅔ cup fresh lemon juice

½ cup sliced almonds

LEMON-CHEESECAKE BARS

⅓ cup butter, softened

¼ cup firmly packed dark brown sugar

¼ tsp. table salt

¼ tsp. ground mace or nutmeg

1 cup plus 2 Tbsp. all-purpose flour, divided

Vegetable cooking spray

1 cup 1% low-fat cottage cheese

1 cup granulated sugar

1 Tbsp. loosely packed lemon zest

3½ Tbsp. fresh lemon juice

¼ tsp. baking powder

1 large egg

1 large egg white

Hands-on 20 min. Total 9 hours, 35 min.

Cottage cheese is the surprise ingredient in these sweet and tart bars, spiced with fragrant mace. Mace is the lacy outer coating of the nutmeg seed, while nutmeg is the kernel inside the seed. They have unique flavors but are often used interchangeably.

1. Preheat oven to 350°F. Beat first 4 ingredients at medium speed with an electric mixer until smooth. Add 1 cup flour, beating at low speed until blended. Press mixture onto bottom of a lightly greased (with cooking spray) 8-inch square pan.

2. Bake at 350°F for 20 minutes.

3. Meanwhile, process cottage cheese in a food processor 1 minute or until smooth, stopping to scrape down sides as needed. Add granulated sugar, remaining 2 Tbsp. flour, lemon zest, and next 4 ingredients; process 30 seconds or until blended. Pour filling over crust.

4. Bake at 350°F for 25 minutes or until set. (Edges will be lightly browned.) Cool 30 minutes. Cover and chill 8 hours. Cut into bars.

MAKES 9 bars

COOKIE SWAP

Use fresh orange or lime juice and zest instead of lemon for a different flavor profile.

TEQUILA-LIME-COCONUT MACAROON BARS

HANDS-ON 20 MIN. TOTAL 2 HOURS, 5 MIN.

Like a fruity beach cocktail in solid form, these refreshing little bites are spiked with tequila. Substitute fresh Key lime juice when available.

1. Preheat oven to 350°F. Line bottom and sides of a 13- x 9-inch pan with heavy-duty aluminum foil, allowing 2 to 3 inches to extend over sides; lightly grease foil with cooking spray.

2. Combine 1¾ cups flour and ½ cup sugar in a medium bowl. Cut in butter with a pastry blender or fork until crumbly. Press mixture onto bottom of prepared pan.

3. Bake at 350°F for 20 to 23 minutes or just until lightly browned.

4. Meanwhile, whisk eggs in a medium bowl until smooth; whisk in coconut, next 3 ingredients, and remaining 1½ cups sugar. Combine remaining ¼ cup flour, baking powder, and salt in a small bowl; whisk flour mixture into egg mixture. Pour filling over hot crust.

5. Bake at 350°F for 25 minutes or until filling is set. Cool in pan 1 hour on a wire rack. Lift from pan, using foil sides as handles. Gently remove foil, and cut into bars.

MAKES 2 dozen bars

INGREDIENTS

Vegetable cooking spray

2 cups all-purpose flour, divided

2 cups sugar, divided

½ cup cold butter, cut into pieces

4 large eggs

1½ cups sweetened flaked coconut

1 tsp. loosely packed lime zest

⅓ cup fresh lime juice

3 Tbsp. tequila

½ tsp. baking powder

¼ tsp. table salt

PEPPERMINT DIVINITY BARS

INGREDIENTS

3 cups all-purpose flour

1 Tbsp. baking powder

1 tsp. kosher salt

Parchment paper

Vegetable cooking spray

1 vanilla bean

1¼ cups butter, softened

2 cups sugar, divided

¼ cup light corn syrup

2 large egg whites

1 tsp. vanilla extract

¼ tsp. peppermint extract

¾ cup crushed hard peppermint candies, divided

HANDS-ON 50 MIN. TOTAL 2 HOURS, 10 MIN.

Spread the warm divinity onto a still-warm cookie base quickly. If too cool, it will tear the base as you spread it.

1. Preheat oven to 375°F. Stir together first 3 ingredients. Line bottom and sides of a 13- x 9-inch pan with parchment paper, allowing 2 to 3 inches to extend over sides; lightly grease (with cooking spray) parchment paper.

2. Split vanilla bean lengthwise, and scrape out seeds into bowl of a heavy-duty electric stand mixer. Add butter and 1 cup sugar; beat at medium speed 2 minutes or until creamy. Add flour mixture, and beat until blended. Press dough into bottom of prepared pan. Bake at 375°F for 20 minutes.

3. Meanwhile, stir together corn syrup, ¼ cup water, and remaining 1 cup sugar in a small saucepan over high heat, stirring just until sugar dissolves. Cook, until a candy thermometer registers 250°F, about 7 to 8 minutes. (Do not stir.)

4. While syrup cooks, beat egg whites at medium speed, using whisk attachment, until foamy. When syrup reaches 250°F, beat egg whites at medium-high speed until soft peaks form. Gradually pour hot sugar syrup into egg whites, beating first at medium speed and then at high speed. Beat until stiff peaks form. (Mixture should still be warm.) Add extracts, beating at medium speed just until combined. Fold in ½ cup peppermint candies.

5. Working quickly, spread mixture on warm cookie base, using a butter knife or offset spatula. Sprinkle with remaining ¼ cup crushed peppermints, and cool.

6. Lift from pan, using parchment paper sides as handles. Remove parchment paper, and cut into bars.

MAKES 32 bars

AMBROSIA STREUSEL BARS

HANDS-ON 30 MIN. TOTAL 2 HOURS, 10 MIN.

The retro fruity Southern salad becomes a delicious topping for these streusel-topped dessert bars. Use the foil as a handle to remove the cooled batch from the pan for easy slicing and cleanup.

1. Preheat oven to 400°F. Line a 13- x 9-inch pan with aluminum foil, extending foil over sides. Butter and flour foil.

2. Prepare Crust: Pulse first 4 ingredients in a food processor 2 to 3 times or until combined; add 1¼ cups cold butter pieces, 2 or 3 pieces at a time, pulsing after each addition. Add egg yolks, 1 at a time, pulsing after each addition. Process until mixture is crumbly. Press mixture onto bottom of prepared pan.

3. Bake at 400°F for 12 minutes or until lightly browned.

4. Prepare Filling: Pulse pineapple in food processor until coarsely chopped. Bring pineapple, marmalade, and next 4 ingredients to a boil in a saucepan over medium-high heat. Boil, stirring often, 1 minute. Remove from heat; let stand 10 minutes. Stir in cherries, and spread in prepared crust. Top with Streusel Topping.

5. Bake at 400°F for 30 minutes or until golden brown. Cool completely in pan (about 1 hour). Lift from pan, using foil sides as handles. Cut into bars.

MAKES 1 to 1¼ dozen

STREUSEL TOPPING

Stir together **½ cup granulated sugar**, **½ cup all-purpose flour**, and **⅛ tsp. kosher salt** in a small bowl. Cut in **3 Tbsp. cold butter, cut into pieces**, until it resembles coarse meal. Stir in **1 cup toasted coconut chips**.

INGREDIENTS

Crust:

2½ cups all-purpose flour

½ cup powdered sugar

½ tsp. kosher salt

½ tsp. baking powder

1¼ cups cold butter, cut into pieces

2 large egg yolks

Filling:

1½ cups fresh pineapple chunks

1 cup orange marmalade

2 Tbsp. granulated sugar

2 Tbsp. fresh lemon juice

2 tsp. cornstarch

¼ tsp. kosher salt

½ cup drained maraschino cherries, coarsely chopped

Streusel Topping

APPLE HELLO DOLLY BARS

Hello Dolly Bar fans will love this fresh twist that uses chopped apples, butterscotch morsels, plenty of crunchy pecans, and toasted coconut. Everyone will rave about this new spin on the classic seven-layer bars—and they'll be gone before you know it!

1. Preheat oven to 350°F. Combine graham cracker crumbs and butter in a small bowl; press onto bottom of a lightly greased (with cooking spray) 13- x 9-inch pan. Layer semisweet chocolate morsels and next 4 ingredients (in order of ingredients list) in prepared pan; drizzle with sweetened condensed milk.

2. Bake at 350°F for 40 to 45 minutes or until deep golden brown. Cool completely in pan on a wire rack (about 1 hour). Cut into bars.

MAKES about 2 dozen bars

SMART COOKIE

Also called seven-layer bars or magic bars, how this sweet confection came to be known as "Hello Dolly Bars" is debatable. First published in the 60s when the musical "Hello Dolly" was all the rage, one column in which the recipe appeared credits Texan Alecia Leigh Couch with the name.

INGREDIENTS

2 cups graham cracker crumbs

½ cup butter, melted

Vegetable cooking spray

½ (12-oz.) package semisweet chocolate morsels

½ (12-oz.) package butterscotch morsels

1 cup sweetened flaked coconut

2 cups peeled and finely chopped Granny Smith apples (about 1 lb.)

1½ cups coarsely chopped pecans

1 (14-oz.) can sweetened condensed milk

APPLE-BUTTERSCOTCH BROWNIES

HANDS-ON 15 MIN. TOTAL 2 HOURS

Some say "butterscotch" originated in Scotland as the name suggests, while others say it refers to the "scotched" or scorched butter that it is made from. Derivation aside, it's a delicious flavoring that has endured.

1. Preheat oven to 350°F. Combine brown sugar and next 3 ingredients in a large bowl.

2. Combine flour and next 2 ingredients in a medium bowl; add flour mixture to brown sugar mixture, stirring until blended. Stir in apples and pecans. Pour mixture into a greased (with shortening) and floured 13- x 9-inch pan; spread in an even layer.

3. Bake at 350°F for 35 to 45 minutes or until a wooden pick inserted in center comes out clean. Cool completely in pan (about 1 hour). Cut into bars.

MAKES about 2 dozen bars

INGREDIENTS

2 cups firmly packed dark brown sugar

1 cup butter, melted

2 large eggs, lightly beaten

2 tsp. vanilla extract

2 cups all-purpose flour

2 tsp. baking powder

½ tsp. table salt

3 cups peeled and diced Granny Smith apples (about 1½ lb.)

1 cup toasted chopped pecans

Shortening

Garnish: sweetened whipped cream

Vegetable cooking spray

Crust:

2 cups all-purpose flour

⅔ cup powdered sugar

¾ cup butter, cubed

Filling:

½ cup firmly packed brown sugar

½ cup honey

⅔ cup butter

3 Tbsp. whipping cream

3½ cups toasted coarsely chopped pecans

Caramel Sauce (optional)

CARAMEL-PECAN BARS

HANDS-ON 40 MIN. TOTAL 2 HOURS, 15 MIN.

Enjoy a handheld version of holiday pecan pie topped with a gooey caramel sauce to add more decadence.

1. Preheat oven to 350°F. Line bottom and sides of a 13- x 9-inch pan with heavy-duty aluminum foil, allowing 2 to 3 inches to extend over sides; lightly grease foil with cooking spray.

2. Prepare Crust: Pulse flour, powdered sugar, and ¾ cup butter in a food processor 5 to 6 times or until mixture resembles coarse meal. Press mixture onto bottom and ¾ inch up sides of prepared pan.

3. Bake at 350°F for 20 minutes or until lightly browned around edges. Cool completely on a wire rack (about 15 minutes).

4. Prepare Filling: Bring brown sugar and next 3 ingredients to a boil in a 3-qt. saucepan over medium-high heat. Stir in toasted pecans. Pour hot filling over cooling crust.

5. Bake at 350°F for 25 to 30 minutes or until golden and bubbly. Cool completely in pan on a wire rack (about 30 minutes). Lift baked bars from pan, using foil sides as handles. Gently remove foil, and cut into bars. Drizzle with Caramel Sauce, if desired.

MAKES about 2 dozen bars

CARAMEL SAUCE

Microwave **40 caramels**, **3 Tbsp. whipping cream**, and **¼ tsp. salt** in a 1-qt. microwave-safe bowl at MEDIUM (50% power) 3½ minutes or until smooth, stirring at 1-minute intervals.

PRALINE BARS

Hands-on 20 min. Total 1 hour

These delicate, wafer-thin treats are a nice twist on the Southern classic.

1. Preheat oven to 350°F. Separate each graham cracker sheet into 4 crackers; place in a lightly greased (with cooking spray) 15- x 10-inch jelly-roll pan. Sprinkle chopped pecans over graham crackers.

2. Bring brown sugar and butter to a boil in a saucepan over medium-high heat. Boil 2 minutes. Pour brown sugar mixture evenly over graham crackers in pan.

3. Bake at 350°F for 10 minutes. Immediately transfer graham crackers to parchment paper, and cool completely (about 30 minutes).

4. Microwave semisweet chocolate morsels in a microwave-safe bowl at HIGH 1 minute or until melted and smooth, stirring at 30-second intervals. Drizzle chocolate evenly over cooled bars. Repeat procedure with white chocolate morsels.

MAKES 5 dozen bars

SMART COOKIE

Pecans are the nut crop of a type of hickory. While these nuts are native to the Mississippi valley area of the U.S., Texas and Georgia are the largest producers of commercial pecans in the country. Pecans are the official nut of Alabama, and the tree is the official tree of the Lone Star State.

INGREDIENTS

15 graham cracker sheets

Vegetable cooking spray

¾ cup chopped pecans

1¾ cups firmly packed brown sugar

1 cup butter

Parchment paper

½ cup semisweet chocolate morsels

½ cup white chocolate morsels

MRS. CLAUS'S DREAM BARS

2 cups gingersnap crumbs

½ cup butter, melted

Shortening

1 (14-oz.) can sweetened condensed milk

1 (6-oz.) package peanut butter chips

¾ cup miniature candy-coated chocolate pieces

1 cup sweetened flaked coconut (optional)

½ cup chopped pecans

HANDS-ON 20 MIN. TOTAL 1 HOUR, 45 MIN.

Christmas calls for cookie bars, and these incorporate everything from gingersnaps to chocolate candies. How else would Mrs. Claus please all the hungry elves at the North Pole?

1. Preheat oven to 350°F. Combine gingersnap crumbs and melted butter in a medium bowl; press onto bottom of a greased (with shortening) 13- x 9-inch pan. Carefully spread condensed milk over crumb mixture.

2. Combine peanut butter chips and remaining 3 ingredients in a medium bowl. Sprinkle mixture evenly over condensed milk; gently press mixture down.

3. Bake at 350°F for 25 to 30 minutes or until lightly browned. Cool (about 1 hour) in pan on a wire rack. Cut into squares.

MAKES about 2 dozen bars

PARTY PERFECT

These are a colorful treat for kids' birthday parties and baby showers. Choose a single color of candy-coated chocolate pieces for monochromatic impact—blue if it's a boy and pink if it's a girl—to fit the occasion or guest of honor.

CHERRY-FILLED WHITE CHOCOLATE BLONDIES

HANDS-ON 15 MIN. TOTAL 2 HOURS

Sweetly swirled with cherry jam and accented with fragrant coconut and almonds, these bars are worth the indulgence. Plus, they're pretty for giving.

1. Preheat oven to 325°F. Place butter in a saucepan over low heat; cook, stirring occasionally, 1 to 2 minutes or until melted. Remove from heat, and add 1 cup white chocolate morsels. (Do not stir.)

2. Beat eggs at high speed with an electric mixer 2 minutes or until foamy. Gradually add sugar, beating until blended. Add white chocolate mixture and almond extract, stirring until blended. Add flour and salt, stirring just until blended. Spread half of batter into a lightly greased (with cooking spray) and floured 8-inch square pan.

3. Bake at 325°F for 20 minutes or until lightly browned.

4. Place cherry preserves in a small saucepan over low heat; cook, stirring frequently, 1 minute or until melted. Spread evenly over partially baked blondies in pan. Combine coconut, remaining 1 cup white chocolate morsels, and remaining half of batter in a medium bowl; spread over melted cherry preserves, spreading to edges of pan. Sprinkle batter with almonds.

5. Bake at 325°F for 25 minutes or until lightly browned. Cool completely in pan on a wire rack (about 1 hour). Cut into bars.

NOTE: To freeze, tightly wrap baked bars in aluminum foil. Place in a large zip-top plastic freezer bag; seal bag, and freeze up to 2 months. Let thaw at room temperature before cutting.

MAKES 16 bars

INGREDIENTS

½ cup butter

1 (12-oz.) package white chocolate morsels, divided

2 large eggs

½ cup sugar

½ tsp. almond extract

1 cup all-purpose flour

½ tsp. table salt

Vegetable cooking spray

½ cup cherry preserves

½ cup sweetened flaked coconut

½ cup sliced almonds

INGREDIENTS

Cooking spray

1 (4-oz.) bittersweet chocolate baking bar, chopped

¾ cup butter

2 cups sugar

4 large eggs

1½ cups all-purpose flour

1 (1-oz.) bottle red liquid food coloring

1½ tsp. baking powder

1 tsp. vanilla extract

⅛ tsp. table salt

Small-Batch Cream Cheese Frosting

RED VELVET BROWNIES

HANDS-ON 15 MIN. TOTAL 3 HOURS, 10 MIN.

A bite-size version of the classic cake gets frosted with the sweet tang of cream cheese frosting. These are the perfect sweet treat for Valentine's Day or Christmas.

1. Preheat oven to 350°F. Line bottom and sides of a 9-inch square pan with aluminum foil, allowing 2 to 3 inches to extend over sides; lightly grease foil with cooking spray.

2. Microwave chocolate and butter in a large microwave-safe bowl at HIGH 1½ to 2 minutes or until melted and smooth, stirring at 30-second intervals. Whisk in sugar. Add eggs, 1 at a time, whisking just until blended after each addition. Gently stir in flour and next 4 ingredients. Pour mixture into prepared pan.

3. Bake at 350°F for 44 to 48 minutes or until a wooden pick inserted in center comes out with a few moist crumbs. Cool completely in pan on a wire rack (about 2 hours).

4. Lift brownies from pan, using foil sides as handles; gently remove foil. Spread Small-Batch Cream Cheese Frosting on top of cooled brownies, and cut into 16 squares.

MAKES 16 bars

SMALL-BATCH CREAM CHEESE FROSTING

Beat **1 (8-oz.) package softened cream cheese** and **3 Tbsp. softened butter** at medium speed with an electric mixer until creamy. Gradually add **1½ cups powdered sugar** and **⅛ tsp. table salt**, beating until blended. Stir in **1 tsp. vanilla**.

HUMMINGBIRD POWER BARS

HANDS-ON 15 MIN. TOTAL 1 HOUR, 50 MIN.

What could be better than a breakfast that tastes like classic hummingbird cake without the colossal calories? Say "hello" to your new start to the day.

1. Preheat oven to 300°F. Combine oats, cereal, walnuts, banana chips, pineapple, coconut, oat bran, and salt in a small bowl.

2. Microwave brown sugar, honey, corn syrup, olive oil, and vanilla in a large microwave-safe bowl at HIGH 1 minute. Pour brown sugar mixture over oat mixture, stirring to coat. Add egg whites to oat mixture, stirring to combine. Press mixture into a lightly greased (with cooking spray) parchment paper-lined 9-inch square pan.

3. Bake at 300°F for 50 minutes or until browned. Cool completely in pan on a wire rack (about 45 minutes). Cut into 16 squares.

NOTE: We tested with Fiber One for high-fiber cereal.

MAKES 16 bars

⭐ PARTY PERFECT

Include these on your sideboard for a weekend brunch, and serve with Greek yogurt or even milk as a handheld cereal option.

INGREDIENTS

1½ cups uncooked regular oats

1 cup high-fiber cereal

1 cup toasted chopped walnuts

1 cup chopped dried banana chips

½ cup chopped dried pineapple

½ cup unsweetened shredded or flaked coconut

½ cup oat bran

½ tsp. table salt

¼ cup firmly packed light brown sugar

¼ cup honey

2 Tbsp. light corn syrup

2 Tbsp. olive oil

1 tsp. vanilla extract

2 large egg whites lightly beaten

Vegetable cooking spray

Parchment paper

SIMPLE BROWNIES WITH CHOCOLATE FROSTING

INGREDIENTS

1 (4-oz.) unsweetened chocolate baking bar, chopped

¾ cup butter

2 cups sugar

4 large eggs

1 cup all-purpose flour

Shortening

Chocolate Frosting

1½ cups toasted coarsely chopped pecans

Hands-on 15 min. Total 2 hours

Everyone needs an easy but decadent brownie in their recipe repertoire, and this one fits the bill. Change things up by using different kinds of nuts. Toasted walnuts, pistachios, or almonds put an entirely new spin on this fantastic basic.

1. Preheat oven to 350°F. Microwave chocolate and butter in a large microwave-safe bowl at HIGH 1 to 1½ minutes or until melted and smooth, stirring at 30-second intervals. Whisk in sugar and eggs until blended. Whisk in flour. Pour mixture into a greased (with shortening) 13- x 9-inch pan.

2. Bake at 350°F for 25 to 30 minutes or until a wooden pick inserted in center comes out with a few moist crumbs.

3. Pour Chocolate Frosting over warm brownies, and spread to edges. Sprinkle with pecans. Cool (about 1 hour) in pan on a wire rack. Cut into squares.

MAKES 4 dozen bars

CHOCOLATE FROSTING

Place **½ cup butter, ⅓ cup sugar,** and **6 Tbsp. unsweetened cocoa** over medium heat in a large saucepan; cook, stirring constantly, 4 to 5 minutes or until butter is melted. Remove from heat, and beat in **1 tsp. powdered sugar** and **1 tsp. vanilla extract** at medium speed with an electric mixer until smooth.

TEX-MEX BROWNIES

Hands-on 25 min. Total 2 hours, 20 min.

These are not your mama's brownies. The subtle heat from red pepper turns these delights into conversation starters with a true Texas bite. Serve with a scoop of vanilla ice cream to tame the flames.

1. Preheat oven to 350°F. Place butter and bittersweet chocolate morsels in a large heavy-duty saucepan over low heat; cook, stirring occasionally, 8 to 10 minutes or until melted and smooth. Remove from heat; cool completely (about 20 minutes).

2. Meanwhile, combine flour and next 4 ingredients in a large bowl until blended; stir in semisweet chocolate morsels.

3. Whisk together granulated sugar and next 3 ingredients until smooth. Whisk in bittersweet chocolate mixture. Add chocolate mixture into flour mixture, whisking just until combined. Line bottom and sides of a 13- x 9-inch pan with parchment paper, allowing 2 to 3 inches to extend over sides; lightly grease parchment (with cooking spray). Pour batter into pan.

4. Bake at 350°F for 35 to 40 minutes or until a wooden pick inserted in center comes out with a few moist crumbs. Cool completely in pan on a wire rack (about 1 hour). Lift brownies from pan, using parchment paper sides as handles. Cut into 24 squares. Dust with more red pepper, if desired.

MAKES 2 dozen bars

INGREDIENTS

1½ cups butter

1 (16-oz.) package bittersweet chocolate morsels

2 cups all-purpose flour

2 tsp. baking powder

1 tsp. ground cinnamon

½ to 1 tsp. ground red pepper, plus more for sprinkling

½ tsp. kosher salt

1 cup semisweet chocolate morsels

1 cup granulated sugar

¾ cup firmly packed dark brown sugar

4 large eggs

1½ Tbsp. vanilla extract

Parchment paper

Vegetable cooking spray

COOKIE SWAP

Texas Sheet Cake Sandwiches: Split each brownie horizontally, and sandwich 1 Tbsp. store-bought chocolate frosting between top and bottom halves.

GERMAN CHOCOLATE-BOURBON-PECAN PIE BARS

HANDS-ON 20 MIN. TOTAL 3 HOURS, 40 MIN.

Admittedly, these are everything-but-the-kitchen-sink bars; but don't discount the downright deliciousness of this bevy of ingredients spiked with a little hair of the dog.

INGREDIENTS

Vegetable cooking spray

Crust:

1¾ cups all-purpose flour

¾ cup powdered sugar

¾ cup cold butter, cubed

¼ cup unsweetened cocoa

1½ cups semisweet chocolate morsels

Filling:

¾ cup firmly packed brown sugar

¾ cup light corn syrup

¼ cup butter, melted

3 large eggs, lightly beaten

¼ cup bourbon

1 cup sweetened flaked coconut

3 cups toasted pecan halves and pieces

1. Preheat oven to 350°F. Line bottom and sides of a 13- x 9-inch pan with heavy-duty aluminum foil, allowing 2 to 3 inches to extend over sides; lightly grease foil (with cooking spray).

2. Prepare Crust: Pulse flour and next 3 ingredients in a food processor 5 to 6 times or until mixture resembles coarse meal. Press mixture on bottom and ¾ inch up sides of prepared pan.

3. Bake at 350°F for 15 minutes. Remove from oven, and sprinkle chocolate morsels over crust. Cool completely on a wire rack (about 30 minutes).

4. Prepare Filling: Whisk together brown sugar and next 3 ingredients in a medium bowl until smooth; whisk in bourbon. Stir in coconut and toasted pecans. Pour filling over cooled crust.

5. Bake at 350°F for 25 to 30 minutes or until golden brown and set. Cool completely in pan on a wire rack (about 1 hour). Chill bars 1 hour. Lift from pan, using foil sides as handles. Gently remove foil, and cut into bars.

MAKES about 2 dozen bars

CAPPUCCINO-FROSTED BROWNIES

HANDS-ON 20 MIN. TOTAL 1 HOUR

People will line up for these brownies gilded with coffee goodness and a sprinkling of chocolate-covered espresso beans.

1. Preheat oven to 350°F. Microwave chocolate squares and butter in a large microwave-safe bowl at HIGH 1½ minutes or until melted and smooth, stirring at 30-second intervals or until melted and smooth. Whisk in sugar. Add eggs, 1 at a time, whisking just until blended after each addition. Whisk in flour and vanilla. Add chocolate morsels, stirring to combine.Pour mixture into a lightly greased (with cooking spray) 13- x 9-inch baking pan.

2. Bake at 350°F for 30 to 35 minutes or until a wooden pick inserted in center comes out clean. Cool completely on pan on a wire rack (about 1 hour).

3. Spread Cappuccino-Buttercream Frosting evenly on top of cooled brownies, and cut into squares. Cover and chill, if desired.

MAKES 1 dozen bars

CAPPUCCINO-BUTTERCREAM FROSTING

Dissolve **1 (1.16-oz.) envelope instant mocha cappuccino mix** in **¼ cup hot milk** in a small cup, stirring to combine; cool completely. Pour milk mixture into a large bowl; add **½ cup softened butter,** and beat at medium speed with an electric mixer until blended. Gradually add **1 (16-oz.) package powdered sugar,** beating until smooth and fluffy.

4 (1-oz.) unsweetened chocolate baking squares

¾ cup butter

2 cups sugar

4 large eggs

1 cup all-purpose flour

1 tsp. vanilla extract

1 cup semisweet chocolate morsels

Vegetable cooking spray

Cappuccino-Buttercream Frosting

SALTED CARAMEL-PECAN BARS

This is a classic Southern bar recipe updated with a sprinkle of kosher salt.

INGREDIENTS

Vegetable cooking spray

12 graham cracker sheets

1 cup firmly packed brown sugar

¾ cup butter

2 Tbsp. whipping cream

1 tsp. vanilla extract

1 cup toasted chopped pecans

¼ tsp. kosher salt

1. Preheat oven to 350°F. Line a 15- x 10-inch jelly-roll pan with aluminum foil; lightly grease foil with cooking spray. Arrange graham crackers in a single layer in prepared pan, slightly overlapping edges.

2. Bring sugar, butter, and cream to a boil in a medium-size heavy saucepan over medium heat, stirring occasionally. Remove from heat, and stir in vanilla and pecans. Pour mixture over graham crackers, spreading to coat. Bake at 350°F for 10 to 11 minutes or until lightly browned and bubbly.

3. Immediately sprinkle with salt. Transfer bars (on aluminum foil) to wire racks, and cool completely (about 30 minutes). Break into bars.

MAKES 4 dozen bars

COOKIE SWAP

For Chocolate-Pecan-Caramel Bars, prepare recipe as directed through Step 2. Top warm bars with 1 cup dark chocolate morsels. Let stand 3 minutes, and spread chocolate over bars. Proceed with recipe as directed in Step 3. Chill 20 minutes before serving.

PEANUT BUTTER STREUSEL BROWNIES

Hands-on 10 min. Total 2 hours

Streusel topping elevates the timeless chocolate-and-peanut butter combo in these brownies.

1. Preheat oven to 350°F. Line bottom and sides of an 8-inch pan with aluminum foil, allowing 2 to 3 inches to extend over sides; lightly grease foil (with cooking spray).

2. Prepare Brownies: Microwave chocolate squares and butter in a large microwave-safe bowl at HIGH 1½ to 2 minutes or until melted and smooth, stirring at 30-second intervals. Whisk in granulated sugar and brown sugar. Add eggs, 1 at a time, whisking just until blended after each addition. Whisk in flour, vanilla, and salt. Pour mixture into prepared pan.

3. Prepare Streusel: Combine flour, brown sugar, granulated sugar, peanut butter, melted butter, and salt in a medium bowl until blended and crumbly. Sprinkle peanut butter mixture over chocolate mixture.

4. Bake at 350°F for 50 to 54 minutes or until a wooden pick inserted in center comes out with a few moist crumbs. Cool completely in pan on a wire rack (about 1 hour). Lift brownies from pan, using foil sides as handles. Gently remove foil, and cut brownies into 16 squares.

MAKES 16 bars

INGREDIENTS

Brownies:

Vegetable cooking spray

4 (1-oz.) unsweetened chocolate baking squares

¾ cup butter

1½ cups granulated sugar

½ cup firmly packed brown sugar

3 large eggs

1 cup all-purpose flour

1 tsp. vanilla extract

⅛ tsp. table salt

Streusel:

½ cup all-purpose flour

2 Tbsp. light brown sugar

2 Tbsp. granulated sugar

⅓ cup chunky peanut butter

2 Tbsp. butter, melted

⅛ tsp. table salt

PEANUT BUTTER-CANDY BAR BROWNIES

INGREDIENTS

Shortening

1 (16-oz.) package peanut-shaped peanut butter sandwich cookies, crushed

½ cup butter, melted

1 (14-oz.) can sweetened condensed milk

½ cup creamy peanut butter

1 Tbsp. vanilla extract

5 (1.5-oz.) packages chocolate-covered peanut butter cup candies, coarsely chopped

2 (2.1-oz.) chocolate-covered crispy peanut buttery candy bars, coarsely chopped

1 cup semisweet chocolate morsels

½ cup honey-roasted peanuts

½ cup sweetened flaked coconut

HANDS-ON 25 MIN. TOTAL 2 HOURS

Peanut butter sandwich cookies become the crumb crust for these chunky brownie bars loaded with candy bar pieces.

1. Preheat oven to 350°F. Line bottom and sides of a 13- x 9-inch baking pan with aluminum foil, allowing 2 to 3 inches to extend over sides; grease foil with shortening.

2. Combine crushed cookies and butter in a medium bowl. Press crumb mixture into bottom of prepared pan.

3. Bake at 350°F for 6 to 8 minutes.

4. Combine condensed milk, peanut butter, and vanilla in a medium bowl, stirring until smooth.

5. Sprinkle peanut butter cup candies, chopped candy bars, chocolate morsels, peanuts, and coconut over crust. Drizzle condensed milk mixture over coconut.

6. Bake at 350°F for 27 minutes or until lightly browned. Cool completely in pan on a wire rack (about 1 hour). Lift brownies from pan, using foil sides as handles. Gently remove foil, and cut into bars.

MAKES 1½ dozen bars

SMART COOKIE

Two Southern peanut farmers were elected President of the United States—Thomas Jefferson and Jimmy Carter. Today, peanuts are the No. 1 snack nut consumed in the U.S.

CONFECTIONS

THE SCOOP ON PERFECT CONFECTIONS

Secrets to create candy shop-worthy treats

1. For candy-making success, use a candy thermometer for precision.

2. As sugar crystallizes on edge of pan, use a wet pastry brush to wash down pan sides.

3. Adding acid, like lemon juice, inhibits the formation of crystals.

4. Set the bottom of the pan in ice water to stop syrups from cooking.

5. Use a double boiler to melt chocolate. Improvise one with a bowl over a saucepan of simmering water.

6. Copper ions combine with egg protein yielding more stable beaten egg whites. Use a copper bowl, if possible.

SORGHUM MARSHMALLOWS

HANDS-ON 40 MIN. TOTAL 8 HOURS, 50 MIN.

Pillowy and sweetened with flavorful sorghum syrup, these marshmallows can float atop a mug of cocoa or be wrapped up for holiday giving.

1. Sprinkle gelatin over ½ cup cold water in bowl of a heavy-duty electric stand mixer. Stir together granulated sugar, next 2 ingredients, and ½ cup water in a 4½-qt. saucepan over medium-high heat; cover and cook 3 minutes, bringing to a boil. Uncover and boil, stirring often, until syrup thickens and a candy thermometer registers 240°F (about 8 to 12 minutes; lower heat as necessary to prevent mixture from boiling over).

2. Gradually add hot sugar mixture to gelatin mixture, beating mixture at low speed, using whisk attachment, 30 seconds or until blended. Increase speed to high (cover bowl with a towel to prevent splattering); beat 10 to 12 minutes or until mixture cools to room temperature and is thick but still pourable.

3. Whisk together cornstarch and powdered sugar. Dust a buttered 13- x 9-inch baking dish with 1 Tbsp. cornstarch mixture. Pour gelatin mixture into prepared dish; smooth with a lightly greased (with cooking spray) spatula. Dust with 1½ Tbsp. cornstarch mixture. Cover remaining cornstarch mixture tightly, and reserve. Let marshmallow mixture stand, uncovered, in a cool, dry place 8 to 14 hours or until dry enough to release from baking dish and no longer sticky.

4. Invert marshmallow slab onto cutting board; cut into squares (about 1 inch each). Toss squares in reserved cornstarch mixture to coat. Store marshmallows in an airtight container at room temperature up to 2 weeks.

*Cane syrup may be substituted for sorghum syrup.

MAKES 8 to 9 dozen

INGREDIENTS

3 envelopes unflavored gelatin

½ cup cold water

1½ cups granulated sugar

1¼ cups sorghum syrup*

¼ tsp. kosher salt

¼ cup cornstarch

¼ cup powdered sugar

Butter

Vegetable cooking spray

DIVINITY

Don't leave anything to chance when making candy. Choose a sunny day with low humidity, gather your equipment before you begin, and measure ingredients precisely. This will help ensure the divinity is feather-light and tender.

1. Preheat oven to 350°F.

2. Combine sugar, corn syrup, salt, and ½ cup water in a heavy 2-qt. saucepan over low heat, and cook, stirring just until sugar dissolves. Cook until a candy thermometer registers 248°F (firm ball stage). Remove from heat.

3. While syrup cooks, beat egg whites at high speed with an electric mixer until stiff peaks form. Gradually pour half of hot syrup into egg whites in a slow, steady stream, beating constantly at high speed 5 minutes. Cook remaining syrup over medium heat, stirring occasionally, 4 to 5 minutes or until a candy thermometer registers 272°F (soft crack stage). Gradually pour hot syrup and vanilla into egg white mixture in a slow, steady stream, beating constantly at high speed until mixture holds its shape (6 to 8 minutes). Stir in chopped pecans.

4. Working quickly, drop mixture by rounded teaspoonfuls onto greased wax paper. Cool 30 minutes.

MAKES about 1¾ lb.

COOKIE SWAP

For Cherry Divinity, substitute 1 cup chopped red candied cherries for pecans. For Peanut Ripple Divinity, omit pecans, and stir in ½ cup peanut butter morsels and ½ cup chopped dry-roasted peanuts.

INGREDIENTS

2½ cups sugar

½ cup light corn syrup

¼ tsp. salt

2 large egg whites

1 tsp. vanilla extract

1 cup toasted chopped pecans

Wax paper

CITRUS MINTS

Hands-on 30 min. Total 4 hours, 30 min.

Citrus and peppermint combine in a refreshing melt-in-your-mouth mint that is perfect for giving any time of year. This recipe makes a lot of candies, so sharing is a good thing. Use powdered sugar to keep the dough from sticking to your hands.

1. Combine cream cheese and butter in a saucepan over low heat, and cook, stirring constantly, until mixture is smooth. Remove from heat.

2. Gradually add powdered sugar, stirring until blended. Stir in peppermint extract and zests.

3. Divide mixture into 8 equal portions. Roll each portion into a 12-inch-long rope. Cut into ½-inch pieces. Let stand 4 hours.

MAKES about 13 dozen

COOKIE SWAP

For Cream Cheese Candy, prepare recipe as directed, omitting peppermint extract and zests.

INGREDIENTS

4 oz. cream cheese

2 Tbsp. butter

1 (16-oz.) package powdered sugar

¼ tsp. peppermint extract

½ tsp. loosely packed lime zest

½ tsp. loosely packed lemon zest

COCONUT JOYS

INGREDIENTS

½ cup butter

2 cups sifted
powdered sugar

3 cups sweetened
flaked coconut

⅓ cup semisweet
chocolate morsels

HANDS-ON 30 MIN. TOTAL 1 HOUR, 30 MIN.

These are simple to make and oh-so-sweet. For a spin on the classic chocolate-almond-coconut candy bar, just press a toasted almond into the coconut balls before drizzling with chocolate.

1. Melt butter in a saucepan over low heat; remove from heat. Stir in sugar and coconut. Shape into ¾-inch balls. Cover and chill 1 hour or until firm.

2. Microwave chocolate morsels in a small microwave-safe bowl at HIGH 30 seconds, or until melted and smooth. Spoon chocolate into a small zip-top plastic freezer bag; seal bag. Snip 1 corner of bag to make a tiny hole. Drizzle a small amount of chocolate over coconut balls. Store in refrigerator.

MAKES 3½ dozen

SMART COOKIE

Sailors aboard Vasco de Gama's ships gave coconuts the name "coco" after the head of a bogeyman due to its hairy appearance and dimpled "eyes." The English added "nut" to the name.

PULLED CANDY

Hands-on 50 min. Total 1 hour, 50 min.

This county fair favorite is fun to make. Sugar is cooked with butter and flavorings, and the mixture is pulled repeatedly into long ropes and twisted as it cools, giving it a shiny opaque color. Saltwater taffy, made popular in the late 1800s in Atlantic City, was given its name because a small amount of saltwater was added to the mixture.

1. Combine sugar, corn syrup, vinegar, and ½ cup water in a large saucepan over medium-low heat; cook, stirring occasionally, 5 to 10 minutes or until sugar dissolves. Using a pastry brush dipped in hot water, brush down any sugar crystals on sides of pan. Cook until a candy thermometer registers 270°F (soft crack stage), about 25 minutes (do not stir). Remove from heat.

2. Add orange or peppermint extract and food coloring. Pour into a buttered 15- x 10-inch jelly-roll pan. Let stand 30 minutes.

3. With buttered hands, pull candy until porous and light colored (about 30 minutes). Cut into small pieces with buttered kitchen shears. Wrap in wax paper.

MAKES about 9 dozen

SMART COOKIE

Tips for pulling candy:
• When candy is cool enough to handle, pull it with buttered hands until it lightens in color, becomes more elastic, and springs back. (Look for parallel ridges that will form on the surface.)
• When candy is ready for cutting, pull it into a rope about ½ to ¾ inch in diameter, and cut with buttered shears or a knife.

INGREDIENTS

3 cups sugar

½ cup light corn syrup

¼ cup white vinegar

¼ tsp. orange or peppermint extract

Food coloring

Butter

Wax paper

POTATO CANDY

HANDS-ON 30 MIN. TOTAL 1 HOUR, 30 MIN.

This old-school candy reminds us of divinity and other traditional homemade Southern sweets. The recipe is a testament to the genius of thrifty cooks who based the confection on leftover mashed potatoes.

INGREDIENTS

⅓ cup peeled, cooked, and mashed russet potato, cold (about 1 large potato)

1 Tbsp. milk

1 tsp. vanilla extract

⅛ tsp. table salt

6 to 7 cups powdered sugar

Parchment paper

⅓ cup creamy peanut butter

1. Beat mashed potato and next 3 ingredients at medium speed with a heavy-duty electric mixer 2 minutes. Beat in 6 cups powdered sugar, 1 cup at a time. Add up to 1 cup powdered sugar, 1 Tbsp. at a time, to form dough.

2. Gather dough into a ball; dust with powdered sugar. Roll to ⅛-inch thickness on parchment paper, and cut into a 12- x 10-inch rectangle. Generously sprinkle powdered sugar over dough, and place a piece of parchment paper over rectangle. Invert rectangle; discard parchment paper on top.

3. Spread peanut butter over dough. Starting at 1 long side, tightly roll up candy, jelly-roll fashion, using parchment paper as a guide. Wrap in parchment paper, and freeze 1 hour. Cut into ¼-inch-thick slices, and serve. Refrigerate sliced candy in an airtight container up to 1 week.

MAKES about 3 dozen

BUTTERSCOTCH DROPS

HANDS-ON 15 MIN. TOTAL 35 MIN.

The crunch in this simple three-ingredient treat comes from shoestring potato sticks. Like pretzels or saltines, they add a bit of salty flavor to balance the sweetness.

1. Melt morsels in a saucepan over low heat. Stir in peanuts and potato sticks.

2. Drop mixture by teaspoonfuls onto wax paper, and cool completely (about 20 minutes).

*1 (6-oz.) package peanut butter morsels may be substituted for butterscotch morsels.

MAKES 2½ dozen

SMART COOKIE

Authentic butterscotch candy is created by combining melted butter and dark brown sugar. Unlike caramel, true butterscotch does not contain milk.

1 (6-oz.) package butterscotch morsels*

1 cup dry-roasted peanuts

1 cup shoestring potato sticks, broken into pieces

Wax paper

3½ cups vanilla wafer
crumbs

2 cups powdered sugar

1 cup chopped pecans

½ cup cola soft drink*

2 Tbsp. butter, melted

Cola Frosting

COLA CANDY

HANDS-ON 30 MIN. TOTAL 1 HOUR

This refrigerator candy is similar to bourbon balls, only spiked with cola instead of bourbon to lend broader appeal.

1. Combine first 5 ingredients. Shape mixture into 1-inch balls. Cover and chill at least 30 minutes.

2. Drizzle or dip balls in Cola Frosting; chill until ready to serve.

*Any dark soft drink may be substituted for cola soft drink.

MAKES 2 dozen

COLA FROSTING

Whisk together **¾ cup powdered sugar, ½ tsp. vanilla extract, ½ cup softened butter,** and **⅓ cup cola soft drink** in a medium bowl.

SMART COOKIE

Southerners have long turned to their favorite cola beverage to make sheet cake, brownies, barbecue sauce, and marinades. Carbonated colas were originally flavored with kola nuts, though nowadays they use brand-specific combinations of sugar, citrus oils, tamarind, cinnamon, vanilla, and an acidic ingredient.

PRALINE PECANS

Unlike the sweet shards of pecan-studded candy that are traditional Southern pralines, these nuts get a crunchy praline coating to make a perfectly bite-size treat for cocktail hour or snacking. Be sure to use a heavy saucepan, and work quickly when spooning the pecan mixture onto the wax paper.

1. Bring first 5 ingredients to a boil in a heavy 3-qt. saucepan over medium heat, stirring constantly. Boil, stirring constantly, 7 to 8 minutes or until a candy thermometer registers 234°F.

2. Remove from heat, and vigorously stir in pecans. Spoon pecan mixture onto wax paper, spreading in an even layer. Let stand 20 minutes or until firm.

3. Break mixture apart into small pieces. Store in an airtight container at room temperature up to 1 week. Freeze in an airtight container or zip-top plastic freezer bag up to 1 month.

MAKES about 8 cups

PARTY PERFECT

These bite-size candied pecans are delicious for snacking and garnishing salads or sweet potato casserole. Package them in vintage paper-lined tins for giving—and to keep moisture out.

INGREDIENTS

1½ cups granulated sugar

¾ cup firmly packed brown sugar

½ cup butter

½ cup milk

2 Tbsp. corn syrup

5 cups toasted pecan halves

Wax paper

SOUTHERN PRALINES

INGREDIENTS

2 cups sugar

2 cups pecan halves

¾ cup buttermilk

2 Tbsp. butter

⅛ tsp. table salt

¾ tsp. baking soda

Parchment paper

Hands-on 30 min. Total 40 min.

Pralines are the South's most iconic candy. These irresistible nuggets of caramel and pecans aren't difficult to make, and the requirements are few: plenty of stirring, patience, and careful attention. A candy thermometer is key to the success of this classic sweet.

1. Combine first 5 ingredients in a large heavy saucepan over low heat; cook, stirring occasionally, 10 minutes or until sugar dissolves. Cook, stirring constantly, until a candy thermometer registers 235°F (soft ball stage).

2. Remove from heat, and stir in baking soda. Beat with a wooden spoon just until mixture begins to thicken. Working quickly, drop mixture by tablespoonfuls onto parchment paper. Let stand at least 30 minutes or until firm.

MAKES 1½ to 2 dozen

SMART COOKIE

This delectable Louisiana brittle candy dates back to 1750. Originally, the patty-shaped, fudge-like delicacy was made with almonds—the preferred nut of the French—and was considered an aid to digestion at the end of a meal. However, the Creoles quickly found a better alternative in the abundant pecan and replaced the white sugar with brown. Today it's considered one of the paramount sweets in the South, particularly in Texas and Louisiana.

"P" NUT BRITTLE

Hands-on 45 min. Total 1 hour, 15 min.

Georgia is known for its peanut crop. The locals like to eat raw unroasted peanuts in the fall and use them in peanut brittle during the holidays. We added pistachios to the mix for a unique new spin on a Southern favorite.

1. Preheat oven to 250°F. Lightly butter a 15- x 10-inch jelly-roll pan. Heat pan in oven 5 minutes.

2. Combine sugar and syrup in a large heavy saucepan over medium-low heat; cook, stirring occasionally, 25 minutes or until mixture starts to bubble and a candy thermometer registers 240°F (soft ball stage). Cover and cook 2 to 3 minutes to wash down sugar crystals from sides of pan (do not stir).

3. Add peanuts and pistachios; cook over medium-low heat until candy thermometer registers 300°F (hard crack stage), about 25 minutes (do not stir). Remove from heat. Carefully stir in baking soda, 1 Tbsp. butter, and vanilla. Spread mixture onto warm pan; and cool completely (about 1 hour). Break into pieces; store cooled brittle in an airtight container in a cool, dry place up to 1 week.

MAKES about 2 lb.

SMART COOKIE

Because there is a day dedicated to everything, mark your calendars: January 26th is "National Peanut Brittle Day."

INGREDIENTS

Butter

2 cups sugar

1 cup light corn syrup

1¼ cups raw peanuts

1¼ cups raw pistachios

½ tsp. baking soda

1 Tbsp. butter

1 tsp. vanilla extract

MATZO TOFFEE BRITTLE

HANDS-ON 15 MIN. TOTAL 1 HOUR, 40 MIN.

Crisp matzo crackers form a delicate base for this caramel-chocolate-almond treat.

INGREDIENTS

Vegetable cooking spray

3½ sheets unsalted matzos

1 cup unsalted butter

1 cup firmly packed light brown sugar

1 cup semisweet chocolate morsels

⅓ cup toasted sliced almonds

1. Preheat oven to 350°F. Line a 15- x 10-inch jelly-roll pan with aluminum foil; lightly grease foil with cooking spray. Arrange matzos in a single layer in prepared pan, breaking as necessary to fit and completely cover bottom of pan.

2. Bring butter and brown sugar to a boil in a small saucepan over medium-high heat, stirring occasionally. Boil, stirring constantly, 3 minutes. Carefully pour mixture evenly over matzos in pan, and spread over matzos.

3. Bake at 350°F for 15 minutes. (Mixture will start to bubble at about 10 minutes. Continue to bake to 15 minutes.) Carefully transfer pan to a wire rack. (Mixture will still be bubbly.) Let stand 1 minute at room temperature or until no longer bubbly. Sprinkle evenly with chocolate morsels; let stand 1 minute or until morsels soften. Spread morsels over brittle; sprinkle with almonds. Let stand 30 minutes.

4. Chill brittle 30 minutes or until chocolate is firm. Break into about 20 pieces. Refrigerate in an airtight container up to 1 week.

NOTE: We tested with Manischewitz Unsalted Matzos.

MAKES about about 1½ lb.

PARTY PERFECT

A welcome treat on the Passover table, these rich yet delicate sweets are an ideal end to the holiday meal.

ALMOND TOFFEE

Hands-on 10 min. Total 1 hour, 30 min.

This crisp candy melts into buttery richness in the mouth, making it an enduring favorite for generations of sweet tooths. Try Southern-made chocolate like Olive & Sinclair.

1. Spread 1 cup almonds into a 9-inch circle on a lightly greased (with cooking spray) baking sheet.

2. Bring sugar, butter, corn syrup, and ¼ cup water to a boil in a heavy saucepan over medium heat; cook, stirring constantly, until golden brown and a candy thermometer registers 290°F to 310°F (about 15 minutes). Carefully pour mixture evenly over almonds on baking sheet. Cool; break into pieces.

3. Microwave chocolate morsels in a small bowl at HIGH 1 minute or until melted and smooth, stirring after 30 seconds. Dip half of each toffee piece into melted chocolate; sprinkle with remaining chopped almonds. Chill 30 minutes or until chocolate is firm. Store in an airtight container up to 1 week.

MAKES about 1½ lb.

Vegetable cooking spray

1½ cups chopped toasted slivered almonds, divided

1 cup sugar

1 cup butter

1 Tbsp. light corn syrup

1 cup semisweet or milk chocolate morsels

24 saltine crackers

1 cup butter

1 cup firmly packed
light brown sugar

1 (12-oz.) package milk
chocolate morsels

½ cup chopped nuts,
such as pistachios,
pecans, or walnuts

SALTINE CRACKER CANDY

HANDS-ON 25 MIN. TOTAL 2 HOURS, 25 MIN.

*Many of us will remember making this candy as children.
It sounds peculiar, but it is really good, especially if you
like the combination of salty and sweet.*

1. Preheat oven to 325°F. Line bottom of a 13- x 9-inch baking pan
with aluminum foil. Arrange crackers in a single layer in pan.

2. Microwave butter and brown sugar in a microwave-safe glass
bowl at HIGH for 3 to 4 minutes or until sugar dissolves, stirring
occasionally. Carefully pour butter mixture evenly over crackers;
spread to coat.

3. Bake at 325°F for 15 minutes or until bubbly. Remove from
oven. Sprinkle evenly with chocolate morsels; let stand 30 seconds
or until morsels soften. Spread morsels over candy; sprinkle with
chopped nuts.

4. Cover and chill candy at least 2 hours. Cut into bars or break
into pieces. Refrigerate in an airtight container.

MAKES about 1 dozen bars

SMART COOKIE

*The saltine was released in 1876 by Nabisco with the slogan "Polly wants
a cracker," but didn't become hugely popular until the Great Depression.
The precisely placed holes are created when the thin
dough is docked to allow steam to escape during baking, yielding a
crispy cracker.*

PUMPKIN FUDGE

Hands-on 25 min. Total 2 hours, 25 min.

These sweet little pumpkin fudge bites feature canned pumpkin, white chocolate, and marshmallow crème.

1. Bring first 6 ingredients to a boil in a 3½-qt. saucepan over medium-high heat, stirring constantly. Cook, stirring constantly, until a candy thermometer registers 234°F (soft ball stage), about 12 minutes.

2. Remove pan from heat; add next 5 ingredients, stirring until blended. Pour mixture into prepared pan. Let stand 2 hours or until cooled completely. Cut into squares or into desired shapes using cookie cutters.

MAKES about 3 lb.

SMART COOKIE

For easy removal, line the pan with aluminum foil before you begin to cook the fudge. Once the candy thermometer reaches 234°F and the remaining ingredients are added, quickly spoon the fudge into the pan. Cool completely so that the fudge is set before cutting into squares.

INGREDIENTS

Shortening

3 cups sugar

¾ cup butter, melted

⅔ cup evaporated milk

½ cup canned pumpkin

2 Tbsp. light corn syrup

1 tsp. pumpkin
pie spice

1 (12-oz.) package white
chocolate morsels

1 (7-oz.) jar
marshmallow crème

1 cup toasted
chopped pecans

1 tsp. vanilla extract

Garnish: toasted
chopped pecans

CHERRY–EGGNOG FUDGE

Christmas isn't complete without a dose of eggnog. This festive holiday fudge, dotted with bits of cherry red, incorporates the rich flavor of the festive boozy drink in an already classic holiday sweet for giving.

1. Line an 8- x 4-inch loaf pan with aluminum foil; butter foil.

2. Bring sugar and next 3 ingredients to a boil in a 4-qt. heavy saucepan over medium heat, stirring constantly. Using a pastry brush dipped in hot water, brush down any sugar crystals on sides of pan. Cook, stirring occasionally, until thermometer registers 238°F. Remove from heat.

3. Let mixture stand until candy thermometer reaches 190°F (15 to 18 minutes). Stir in pecans and remaining 3 ingredients; beat with a wooden spoon until fudge thickens and just begins to lose its gloss (5 to 8 minutes).

4. Pour mixture into prepared pan. Let stand 2 hours or until cooled completely. Cut into squares.

MAKES 1½ lb.

INGREDIENTS

Butter

2 cups sugar

1 cup refrigerated eggnog

2 Tbsp. butter

2 Tbsp. light corn syrup

¼ cup toasted chopped pecans

¼ cup toasted slivered almonds, chopped

½ cup chopped red candied cherries

1 tsp. vanilla extract

HOMEMADE CARAMEL TAFFY

Hands-on 35 min. Total 2 hours, 35 min.

A gift of Homemade Caramel Taffy will be a sure hit for the caramel connoisseur on your list.

1. Line bottom and sides of an 8-inch square pan with aluminum foil, allowing 2 to 3 inches to extend over sides; generously grease foil with shortening.

2. Melt 1 cup butter in a 3-qt. saucepan over low heat. Add in brown sugar, sweetened condensed milk, and corn syrup until smooth. Bring to a boil. Cook over medium heat, stirring constantly, until a candy thermometer registers 235°F (about 20 minutes). Remove from heat.

3. Add orange zest; stir 1 minute or until mixture is smooth and no longer bubbling. Quickly pour mixture into prepared pan. Let stand 2 hours or until completely cooled.

4. Lift caramels from pan, using foil sides as handles. Cut into 2- x 1-inch pieces with a buttered knife. Wrap each piece in wax paper or a taffy wrapper. Store at room temperature up to 1 week.

MAKES about 2½ dozen

⭐ PARTY PERFECT

Waxed taffy wrappers protect homemade taffy from humidity without sticking to candy. Find the wrappers online in solids and patterns to fit the occasion.

INGREDIENTS

Shortening

1 cup butter

1 (16-oz.) package dark brown sugar

1 (14-oz.) can sweetened condensed milk

1 cup light corn syrup

1 Tbsp. loosely packed orange zest

Wax paper

CHERRY-PISTACHIO BARK

HANDS-ON 15 MIN. TOTAL 1 HOUR, 15 MIN.

Bark is a sheet candy often made from chocolate and nuts. This recipe uses white chocolate and crunchy pistachios, making it perfect for holiday giving.

1. Line a 15- x 10-inch jelly-roll pan with parchment paper. Microwave cherries and 2 Tbsp. water in a small glass bowl at HIGH 2 minutes; drain.

2. Melt white chocolate morsels and candy coating in a heavy saucepan over low heat. Remove from heat; stir in half of cherries and half of pistachios. Spread mixture into prepared pan. Sprinkle with remaining half of cherries and half of pistachios.

3. Chill 1 hour or until firm. Cut or break into pieces. Store in an airtight container.

MAKES 3½ lb.

SMART COOKIE

Bark is similar to brittle in that it's a thin sheet of candy easily broken into pieces. However, bark is traditionally made of chocolate with any number of things embedded in it—nuts, dried fruit, pretzels, or candies. It got its name from its resemblance to the rough bark of a tree.

INGREDIENTS

Parchment paper

1¼ cups dried cherries

2 (12-oz.) packages white chocolate morsels

6 (2-oz.) vanilla candy coating squares

1¼ cups chopped red or green pistachios

CHOCOLATE-DIPPED PRALINE PRETZELS

Hands-on 20 min. Total 1 hour, 5 min.

Fun to make and fun to eat, these sweet-and-salty batons are great treats for giving.

1. Preheat oven to 350°F. Combine pecans, brown sugar, and cream in a medium bowl. Spread mixture in a single layer in a lightly buttered 9-inch round cake pan.

2. Bake at 350°F for 20 minutes or until sugar is slightly crystallized, stirring once. Cool in pan 10 minutes; finely chop. Spread mixture in a single layer on parchment paper.

3. Microwave chocolate in a microwave-safe measuring cup at HIGH 1 minute or until melted, stirring at 15-second intervals. Immediately dip two-thirds of each pretzel rod into chocolate, twirling to coat all sides. Roll coated ends of pretzels in pecan mixture. Gently place on parchment paper; let stand until chocolate is set. Store in airtight containers up to 4 days.

MAKES 16 pretzels

⭐ PARTY PERFECT

Arranged in a glass or vase on the dessert table or packaged in cellophane sleeves or glass jars for giving, these simple treats are always welcome.

INGREDIENTS

1½ cups coarsely chopped pecans

¼ cup firmly packed light brown sugar

2 Tbsp. heavy cream

Butter

Parchment paper

2 (4-oz.) semisweet chocolate baking bars, chopped

16 pretzel rods

BOURBON BALLS

HANDS-ON 30 MIN. TOTAL 30 MIN.

Bourbon Balls offer up a powerful punch in a small bite. These sweet, no-bake treats are a favored Southern holiday gift and a perfect nibble for parties.

1. Combine vanilla wafers and next 3 ingredients in a large bowl, stirring until blended.

2. Combine bourbon and corn syrup, stirring until blended. Add bourbon mixture to wafer mixture. Shape mixture into 1-inch balls; roll in powdered sugar. Cover and chill up to 2 weeks.

MAKES about 5 dozen

⭐ PARTY PERFECT

For a festive presentation, roll bourbon balls in different coatings, such as candy sprinkles, cookie crumbs, sanding sugars, or cocoa, or drizzle with icing. These make a welcome gift at the holidays or a rich post-meal sweet served with espresso.

INGREDIENTS

1 (12-oz.) package vanilla wafers, finely crushed

1 cup toasted chopped pecans

¾ cup powdered sugar

2 Tbsp. unsweetened cocoa

½ cup bourbon

2½ Tbsp. light corn syrup

Powdered sugar

RASPBERRY-FUDGE TRUFFLES

Hands-on 40 min. Total 3 hours, 40 min.

Summertime preserves add interest to these anytime chocolate confections. Use a sturdy wooden pick to dip well-chilled or frozen balls.

1. Microwave chocolate morsels in a microwave-safe 4-cup glass measuring cup at HIGH 1½ to 2½ minutes or until melted, stirring at 30-second intervals.

2. Beat cream cheese at medium speed with an electric mixer until smooth. Add melted chocolate, preserves, and liqueur, beating until blended. Stir in vanilla wafer crumbs; cover and chill 2 hours.

3. Shape mixture into 1-inch balls; cover and freeze 1 hour or until firm.

4. Microwave chocolate coating in a 4-cup glass measuring cup at HIGH 1½ to 2½ minutes or until melted, stirring at 30-second intervals. Dip balls in coating; place on wax paper.

5. Microwave white chocolate and shortening in a small microwave-safe bowl at HIGH 1 minute or until melted, stirring after 30 seconds. Tint with red food coloring. Spoon mixture into a small zip-top plastic freezer bag; seal bag. Snip 1 corner of bag to make a tiny hole. Drizzle a small amount of chocolate over balls. Let stand 30 minutes or until firm. Store in refrigerator or freezer, if desired.

MAKES 6 dozen

INGREDIENTS

2 cups (12 oz.) semisweet chocolate morsels

2 (8-oz.) packages cream cheese, softened

1 cup seedless raspberry preserves

2 Tbsp. raspberry liqueur

1½ cups vanilla wafer crumbs

10 (2-oz.) chocolate candy coating squares

Wax paper

3 (1-oz.) white chocolate squares

1 Tbsp. shortening

1 to 2 drops red oil-based food coloring

EASY SWIRLED FUDGE

INGREDIENTS

Parchment paper

½ cup butter

1 (16-oz.) package
powdered sugar, sifted

½ cup unsweetened
cocoa

¼ cup milk

¼ tsp. table salt

1 Tbsp. vanilla extract

1 (4-oz.) white
chocolate baking bar,
chopped

2 Tbsp. whipping
cream

HANDS-ON 15 MIN. TOTAL 2 HOURS, 20 MIN.

A very thin crust forms over the surface of the fudge while you microwave the white chocolate mixture. Don't be alarmed—once you swirl the two together, it will become smooth again.

1. Line bottom and sides of an 8-inch square pan with parchment paper, allowing 2 to 3 inches to extend over sides.

2. Microwave butter in a large microwave-safe glass bowl at HIGH for 30-second intervals until melted. Gently stir in powdered sugar and next 3 ingredients. (Mixture will be lumpy.) Microwave at HIGH 30 seconds; stir in vanilla.

3. Beat mixture at medium-low speed with an electric mixer until smooth. Pour mixture evenly into prepared pan.

4. Microwave white chocolate and whipping cream in a small microwave-safe glass bowl at HIGH until white chocolate is melted, stirring after 30 seconds. Stir until mixture is smooth. Let stand 1 to 3 minutes or until slightly thickened. Spoon mixture over fudge in pan, swirling with a knife. Cover and chill until firm (about 2 hours).

NOTE: We tested in a 1,100-watt and a 1,250-watt microwave oven. Cook times will vary depending on your microwave wattage; be sure to follow the descriptions in the recipe for best results.

MAKES about 1¾ lb.

MISSISSIPPI MUD MEDALLIONS

Hands-on 25 min. Total 40 min.

Mississippi mud cakes, pies, and brownies are a chocolate-lover's favorites. You can swap the marshmallows for chocolate-covered espresso beans for an eye-opening change of pace.

1. Place 3 graham cracker sheets in a zip-top plastic freezer bag, and roll with a rolling pin until finely crushed. Spoon crushed graham crackers by level ½ teaspoonfuls 1 inch apart onto a parchment paper-lined baking sheet; flatten into 1-inch rounds. Break remaining crackers into ½-inch pieces.

2. Microwave chocolate morsels in a microwave-safe bowl at HIGH 30 seconds; stir. Microwave 10 to 20 more seconds or until melted and smooth, stirring at 10-second intervals.

3. Spoon melted chocolate into a large zip-top plastic freezer bag. Snip 1 corner of bag to make a small hole. Pipe chocolate over each graham cracker round.

4. Working quickly, gently press 1 (½-inch) graham cracker piece, 1 toasted pecan half, and a few marshmallows onto each chocolate round. Chill 15 minutes. Store in an airtight container at room temperature up to 1 week.

MAKES 3 dozen

INGREDIENTS

6 graham cracker sheets

Parchment paper

2 cups semisweet chocolate morsels

⅔ cup toasted pecan halves

½ cup mini marshmallows

SWEET & SALTY POPCORN SNACK MIX

INGREDIENTS

15 cups popped popcorn
(about ¾ cup kernels)

Vegetable cooking spray

1 cup plus 2 Tbsp.
firmly packed
dark brown sugar

½ cup butter

½ cup dark corn syrup

¼ tsp. kosher salt

1 cup lightly salted
dry-roasted peanuts

Wax paper

1 (10.5 oz.) package
candy-coated
peanut butter pieces

HANDS-ON 30 MIN. TOTAL 1 HOUR

There's no trick to this treat. All you need is 30 minutes to make this scary-good mix for a Halloween party or your next movie night.

1. Preheat oven to 325°F. Spread popcorn in an even layer on a lightly greased (with cooking spray) heavy-duty aluminum foil-lined 13- x 18-inch pan.

2. Combine brown sugar and next 3 ingredients in a small saucepan over medium-low heat; simmer, stirring constantly, 1 minute. Pour over popcorn, and stir gently to coat.

3. Bake at 325°F for 25 minutes, stirring every 5 minutes. Add peanuts during last 5 minutes. Remove from oven, and spread on lightly greased (with cooking spray) wax paper. Cool completely (about 20 minutes). Break apart large pieces, and stir in candy pieces. Store in an airtight container up to 1 week.

MAKES about 17 ½ cups

★ PARTY PERFECT

The salty, sweet snack is great for any occasion. Use red and green candy-coated chocolate pieces at Christmas, red cinnamon candies at Valentine's Day, and pastel-coated candies at Easter or for baby or bridal showers.

GIVE A COOKIE GUIDE

Everyone enjoys receiving yummy food gifts during the holidays or any time of the year. Make your presents look as good as they taste with these easy cookie-packaging ideas.

GOT COOKIES?

Fill a mug or decorative drinking glass with cookies, add a striped paper straw and package in cellophane. Include a gift tag to remind guests that baked goodies are even better dunked in an ice-cold glass of milk.

PANTRY PACKAGING

Load up Mason jars with sweets and attach a cute printed label to the top or side of the jar. Fill a paper sack with treats, fold over the top, punch two holes just below the crease, weave ribbon through, and tie. Stack cookies and roll up in wax paper. Twist the ends and secure with string.

SWEET KEEPSAKE

Heap cookies into vintage enameled cookie tins (tea tins are the perfect size for a small batch) or small wooden boxes that can be used for storage long after the cookies are gone. Scour tag sales for retro cookie jars too.

COOKIES FOR COOKS

For an edible gift that first can be enjoyed and then made over and over again, bundle a batch of just-baked cookies piled high in a colorful mixing bowl. Wrap it up and attach a wooden spoon along with a recipe card.

SIGN, SEAL, DELIVER

Ensure a sweet—and safe—delivery. Once packaged, tied, and tagged, don't forget to consider allergies. If you are not including a recipe card with your fresh-from-the-oven finest, be sure to highlight ingredients like chocolate, nuts, or wheat flour that can cause a reaction in those susceptible.

COOKIE SWAP SECRETS

Hosting a cookie exchange offers a chance to get together with friends during the busy holiday season and a shortcut to your holiday baking at the same time. It's an easy party to throw, especially when you keep these tips in mind.

PLAN EARLY

Give as much advance notice as possible. Chances are, not everyone you invite will be able to attend. Ask everyone to let you know what type of cookies they'll bring. It's the host's job to keep a running list to avoid duplications. Remind partygoers to bring a few extra empty tins or resealable bags to take their cookies home in.

DETERMINE THE NUMBER OF COOKIES GUESTS SHOULD BRING

Ask each guest to bring 6 dozen cookies from a single recipe and each guest should leave with 6 dozen cookies, no matter how many people attend. Or you can base the number of cookies to bring on the number of guests. If you expect 7 guests, ask each person to bring 8 dozen cookies so everyone will get a full dozen of each cookie variety (including the host).

GET COPIES OF THE RECIPES IN ADVANCE

Each guest should go home with a copy of all of the cookie recipes. Ask guests to e-mail you their recipes a few days ahead of time so you can print them out for guests to take home from the party.

PREPARE SOME SAVORY SNACKS

You and your guests will be sampling lots of cookies, so it's nice to offer some savory snacks and drinks to balance all that irresistable sweetness.

RECICE INDEX

CANDY MAKING

Thread Stage	223° to 234°F	Syrup spins a 2-inch thread when dropped from a metal spoon.
Soft Ball Stage	234° to 240°F	In cold water, syrup forms a soft ball that flattens when removed from water.
Firm Ball Stage	242° to 248°F	In cold water, syrup forms a firm ball that doesn't flatten when removed from water.
Hard Ball Stage	250° to 268°F	Syrup forms a hard, yet pliable, ball when removed from cold water.
Soft Crack Stage	270° to 290°F	When dropped into cold water, syrup separates into threads that are hard but not brittle.
Hard Crack Stage	300° to 310°F	When dropped into cold water, syrup separates into threads that are hard and brittle.
Caramel Stage	310° to 340°F	Syrup will be honey-colored when spooned onto a white plate. The longer it cooks, the darker it becomes.

METRIC EQUIVALENTS

The recipes that appear in this cookbook use the standard U.S. method for measuring liquid and dry or solid ingredients (teaspoons, tablespoons, and cups). The information on this chart is provided to help cooks outside the United States successfully use these recipes. All equivalents are approximate.

METRIC EQUIVALENTS FOR DIFFERENT TYPES OF INGREDIENTS

A standard cup measure of a dry or solid ingredient will vary in weight depending on the type of ingredient. A standard cup of liquid is the same volume for any type of liquid. Use the following chart when converting standard cup measures to grams (weight) or milliliters (volume).

Standard Cup	Fine Powder (ex. flour)	Grain (ex. rice)	Granular (ex. sugar)	Liquid Solids (ex. butter)	Liquid (ex. milk)
1	140 g	150 g	190 g	200 g	240 ml
¾	105 g	113 g	143 g	150 g	180 ml
⅔	93 g	100 g	125 g	133 g	160 ml
½	70 g	75 g	95 g	100 g	120 ml
⅓	47 g	50 g	63 g	67 g	80 ml
¼	35 g	38 g	48 g	50 g	60 ml
⅛	18 g	19 g	24 g	25 g	30 ml

USEFUL EQUIVALENTS FOR LIQUID INGREDIENTS BY VOLUME

¼ tsp					=	1 ml	
½ tsp					=	2 ml	
1 tsp					=	5 ml	
3 tsp	=	1 Tbsp		=	½ fl oz	=	15 ml
		2 Tbsp	=	⅛ cup	=	1 fl oz	=	30 ml
		4 Tbsp	=	¼ cup	=	2 fl oz	=	60 ml
		5⅓ Tbsp	=	⅓ cup	=	3 fl oz	=	80 ml
		8 Tbsp	=	½ cup	=	4 fl oz	=	120 ml
		10⅔ Tbsp	=	⅔ cup	=	5 fl oz	=	160 ml
		12 Tbsp	=	¾ cup	=	6 fl oz	=	180 ml
		16 Tbsp	=	1 cup	=	8 fl oz	=	240 ml
		1 pt	=	2 cups	=	16 fl oz	=	480 ml
		1 qt	=	4 cups	=	32 fl oz	=	960 ml
					33 fl oz	=	1000 ml = 1 l

USEFUL EQUIVALENTS FOR DRY INGREDIENTS BY WEIGHT

(To convert ounces to grams, multiply the number of ounces by 30.)

1 oz	=	¹⁄₁₆ lb	=	30 g
4 oz	=	¼ lb	=	120 g
8 oz	=	½ lb	=	240 g
12 oz	=	¾ lb	=	360 g
16 oz	=	1 lb	=	480 g

USEFUL EQUIVALENTS FOR LENGTH

(To convert inches to centimeters, multiply the number of inches by 2.5.)

1 in				=	2.5 cm	
6 in	=	½ ft		=	15 cm	
12 in	=	1 ft		=	30 cm	
36 in	=	3 ft	=	1 yd	=	90 cm	
40 in				=	100 cm	=	1 m